Day Care and the Public Schools

Profiles of Five Communities

JAMES A. LEVINE

Published by

Education Development Center, Inc.
55 Chapel Street
Newton, Massachusetts 02160

edc

Inquiries about the report
should be directed to:

James A. Levine
Center for Research on Women
Wellesley College
828 Washington Street
Wellesley, Massachusetts 02181
(617) 235-0320, ext. 785 or 781

Copies of the report are available at
$5.00 prepaid, including postage, from:

EDC Distribution Center
39 Chapel Street
Newton, Massachusetts 02160

An edc Book
Editor: Adeline Naiman
Designer: Marianne Boris

Contents

Acknowledgments

Many people and many organizations helped with the preparation of this report.

Financial support came from the Education Division and the National Affairs Division of the Ford Foundation; for their interest, encouragement, and patience, I thank Marjorie Martus and Susan Berresford.

For their cooperation, graciousness, and again, patience, I thank all those people whom I interviewed in the five communities profiled here, as well as in Washington, D.C., which was not included in the final report.

Representatives of virtually every organization which has expressed an opinion about public school prime sponsorship generously provided background information and documents, and many individuals served as invaluable resources during the project. They include Marilyn Rauth of the American Federation of Teachers, Ellen Hoffman and Harley Frankel of the Children's Defense Fund, Peg Jones (then of the National Foundation for the Improvement of Education), Judy Ain, Barbara Tannen, Gil Steiner, Ed Martin, Miles Myers, Micki Seltzer, Gwen Morgan, Nancy Travis, Jackie Cooke, Jill Herold, Jack Hailey, and Edwina Hertzberg.

Special thanks go to Dick Ruopp, who originally encouraged me to devote my attention to this area; to Terry Foudriat, who helped with the research; to Rochelle Beck, Susan Berresford, Norton Grubb, Marjorie Martus, Susan Muenchow, and Mary Rowe, who all gave generously of their time in reviewing and critiquing different drafts of the manuscript; to Adeline Naiman, my editor at EDC, and Marianne Boris, Production Manager; to Julie Hansen, Tracy Sluicer, Jan Putnam, and Ethel Brown, all of whom helped turn my illegible copy into a typed manuscript; and to the Wellesley College Center for Research on Women and its director, Carolyn Elliott, who provided a supportive working atmosphere throughout this project.

I.

Introduction: About This Report

Goals

Much heat but little light has been generated in debate about using the public schools as a provider or sponsor of day care services. Proponents of school-run day care argue that the facilities are in place, elementary classrooms are emptying, and there is a surplus of teachers. Opponents contend that day care is different from schooling, that elementary teachers are not prepared to meet the needs of young children or their families, and that public school control of day care will institutionalize—in the worst sense of the word—the care of small children. Well-defined on each side, the arguments are leading to a not uncommon phenomenon in day care: polarization of interest groups.

For the most part, debate has been cast in rather abstract either-or terms. In proposing presumed prime sponsorship, the American Federation of Teachers (AFT) set forth the advantages of "the schools," in general; opponents have reacted by enumerating all the reasons why "the schools," in general, should not have control of day care. Lacking from most discussion is any examination of the ways in which particular schools or school systems are already involved in day care, how they became involved, and with what consequences.[1]

This report attempts to begin filling the information gap. By profiling public school-affiliated day care in five communities throughout the country, I hope to promote a more constructive dialogue (i.e., one that does not mark out the pros and cons so abstractly and absolutely) among all those who are concerned about, and who might work towards the development of, better services for children and families.

Each program described represents a different type of school involvement with day care. In some, schools are a provider of direct serv-

1

ices; in others, schools have entered into a partnership-contract with parent- or community-controlled nonprofit groups. Selection of these models is *not* meant as an endorsement, or to indicate in any way that I am in favor of presumed prime sponsorship. Rather, each highlights, to some extent, a different dimension of the debate about day care and the public schools; in so doing, each may help give focus to debate at the national and local levels. Included are the following:

Oakland Children's Centers, Oakland, California
(Preschool and After-school Care)
Significant because of its history as the oldest and one of the largest school district operated day care programs in the country, the Oakland Children's Centers program also raises important questions about the future status and costs of public school day care. In 1974, largely because of teacher union activity, credentialed Children's Centers teachers were given a nine-month work year and the same salary schedule as their colleagues in the public schools.

Extended Day Programs, Brookline, Massachusetts
(After-school Care)
After-school day care, now available in all eight of Brookline's elementary schools, represents an interesting model of parent control within the public school system. Each Extended Day Program operates both as a parent-run not-for-profit corporation *and* as an official part of the Brookline Public Schools, following guidelines adopted by the School Committee.

Comprehensive Child Day Care Program, Atlanta, Georgia
(Preschool and After-school Care)
One of the most extensive in the country, this public school day care program serves some 3,535 Title XX children, 64 percent of all Title XX children in Atlanta. However, its underlying rationale is not day care as a social service but day care as a means of early educational intervention. Accordingly, the Atlanta schools place a strong emphasis on the achievement and measurement of educational objectives.

Education for Parenthood Pilot Project, Austin, Texas
(Infant and Toddler Care)
In a unique partnership, the Austin Independent School District is teaming up with Child, Inc., Austin's largest private nonprofit day care agency, to offer day care to some 80 infants and toddlers. Four high school-based Infant and Family Development Centers care for the children while their teen-aged parents attend school; in addition, the centers

serve as laboratories for an Education for Parenthood Project available to all high school students.

Family Day Care in Anderson 5 and Pickens County, South Carolina (Family Day Care)

With 20 of its 92 school districts operating day care programs, South Carolina has an extensive system of school-based day care. More important here, however, is the operation in two different districts—one rural and one suburban—of school-affiliated family day care programs, probably the first in the nation.

In the profile of each of these programs, emphasis is on how the involvement of the public schools developed and on how each particular set of arrangements works: What is the administrative structure? How is the program financed, and how much does it cost? What are the criteria for personnel? In what ways are parents involved? And so forth. That is, emphasis is not on the day to day experience of children but on the organization and dynamics of the total system in which children receive care. The intent here is not to evaluate but to describe accurately and analytically the complexities and trade-offs—the strengths and stresses—within each of the delivery systems.

This is not to say that I don't have personal judgments or overall impressions of programs. During the week to ten days I spent in each community, I could not help but make mental notes of qualitative differences from center to center, differences that so often seemed related to an individual center's leadership.[2] Moreover, my summary and synthesis of "findings," which appears as Chapter V of this report, offers an overview of all the programs in relationship to one another. However, as a former day care director, I was especially sensitive to the "quick and dirty" evaluation, the brief visit by an outsider or so-called "expert" who, after visiting one or two groups of children, praises or damns a whole program. Given the relatively short visits I made to each of these programs and the diversity within—let alone between—programs, I thought it would be presumptuous to make such summary judgments, to claim that certain programs were "good" or "bad."

Because the relationship between day care and the public schools is such a controversial topic, I want, at the outset, to emphasize several caveats and clarify my intentions:

First, this report is intended not to yield simple answers but to generate more attention to complexities. My hope is that a description and analysis of trade-offs within delivery systems will be instructive to those concerned with day care and/or educational policy, and *useful* to those program developers at the community level who, whatever their affiliation, are concerned about both the possibilities and the problems of different types of school involvement in day care.

Second, this report is not meant to imply that the public school issue is or should be *the* central focus of policy development for child care in the years ahead. It is an important issue, one that will continue to command attention, but as Norton Grubb has so aptly pointed out, it provides but one among several alternative perspectives on the development of national child care policy.[3] (Among other perspectives are those that emphasize voucher payments, income transfer policies, and the development of consumer-oriented child care information and referral services.[4])

Third and last, I stress again that this report is not intended—either explicitly or implicitly—to substantiate arguments for public school prime sponsorship of day care. Because the needs, resources, and histories of communities in this country are so diverse, it would seem unwise to assume categorically that the schools (or any other agency) are the best possible sponsor or provider of day care; it would seem equally unwise for national policy to exclude the schools as a potential provider of day care. The variety represented in this report suggests the need for an approach to national day care policy that values pluralism and local planning.

Methods: Site Selection and Information Gathering

This project was designed to profile five or six examples of school-affiliated day care, with day care defined as full-day or after-school programs geared to meet the needs of working parents; this excluded half-day preschool programs and all half-day Head Start programs.

Site selection and preparation of the final report involved the following phases, carried out between September 1976 and December 1977:

Site Identification

Two methods were used to locate examples of school-affiliated day care. Letters were sent to Department of Public Welfare day care licensing staff and to Department of Education early childhood staff in all fifty states, requesting identification of any public school-based or -affiliated day care programs. Follow-up phone calls were made to identified sites to gather more information. Follow-up calls were also made to non-respondent state personnel and to key leaders in the day care and education communities to ensure that the search touched base with all fifty states.

Site Selection

Several factors were considered in selecting sites from those identified in the search:

• **Scope of Service:** Selected communities had to have a "system" of school-affiliated day care. This excluded many communities where one or two schools are involved in some way in providing day care, including two particularly interesting ones.

In Wheat Ridge, Colorado, a suburb of Denver, day care is available at one elementary school (Martensen) on a sliding-fee scale basis to all working parents who live within the school district. Because of the district's open-enrollment policy, a child's education can be coordinated with a working parent's needs: children living out of the Martensen neighborhood simply transfer in for both schooling and day care. Approximately 75 percent of people using the Martensen Children's Center are not from the immediate school neighborhood.

In Lawton, Oklahoma, a specially designated "School for Working Parents" serves a similar function. In Lawton, however, day care is free to all families, regardless of income, because it was established under court order as a mechanism to facilitate racial desegregation.

The "system" criteria also excluded Washington, D.C., which has a variety of school-affiliated day care programs, some under the auspices of the Recreation Department, some operated in connection with Capitol Area Day Care (the city's largest nonprofit day care provider), and some operated by parent groups in individual schools. Initially selected as a site for study, the District's school personnel, day care representatives, and parents were extremely gracious in facilitating a visit. However, the city's programs proved to be too diverse—too "unsystematic"—to profile in this report.

Head Start, too, was excluded under the "system" criteria. Because Head Start has been the most politically viable of all the nation's preschool programs, instances of full-day Head Start programs based in public schools have an inherent national significance. They become even more significant in light of the Carter administration's endorsement in April 1978 of a bill (S.991), introduced by Connecticut Senator Abraham Ribicoff, that would establish a separate cabinet level Department of Education, with authority over Head Start.* However, there are no available statistics on the number of full-day school-based Head Starts, and as far as I could ascertain, there are no communities in which full-day Head Start affiliated with public schools constitutes a system.[5]

---

*On July 11, 1978, as this report was going to press, the Senate Governmental Affairs Committee unanimously voted against putting Head Start in the proposed Department of Education.

• **Administrative, Fiscal, and Operational Arrangements:** Each community selected had to represent a distinctive type of public school day care arrangement. According to this criterion, the inclusion of after-school day care in Brookline because of its distinctive parent control meant excluding a number of other after-school programs of larger scope, such as Arlington and Alexandria, Virginia, and Portland, Oregon.

The selection of a community because of its particular approach does not imply endorsement of that approach. Nor is selection meant to indicate that any of these communities is "typical," i.e., representative of some larger set of very similar communities. Rather, each represents and highlights a set of issues in the controversy over public school involvement in day care.

• **Willingness to Participate:** Naturally, all sites selected had to be willing to participate in this study. The only selected site which declined inclusion was Philadelphia, Pennsylvania, where the public schools operate two extensive and different day care programs (a Title XX Get Set and a separate Board of Education child care program, which dates back over 30 years) and where the AFT has been particularly active in organizing day care teachers.

• **Geographical Distribution:** Consideration was also given to geographical distribution. This meant, for example, choosing only one of the many Children's Centers programs in California.

Gathering of Information

Site visits of approximately one to two weeks duration were made to all of the profiled communities between November 1976 and June 1977. During that time I spoke with central administrative staff, day care directors, teachers, parents, union officials, and interested members of the day care community. Interviews were of no set length but were designed so that I could gather input from all major actors in the scene and develop a balanced view of how school-related day care worked in each community. Considerable follow-up with interviewees was done via telephone calls and correspondence. In addition, I reviewed printed material available at each of the sites.

Review of Draft Profiles

Draft profiles were sent for review to all major sources of information, and I took their comments and corrections into account in making revisions for the final manuscript.

It must be stressed that profiles reflect the status of programs at the time of site visits, all of which were conducted between November 1976 and June 1977. However, as of April 1978, when final revisions of this report were made, Atlanta's Comprehensive Child Care Program was the only one of the programs that had made, or that was about to make, a major change in any of its key programmatic elements. (In addition, the recent passage of "Proposition 13" in California will undoubtedly have important implications for the Oakland Children's Centers—changes which are not reflected in this report.) The change in Atlanta, which regards personnel policies, and minor changes in some of the other sites, are noted in the introductions to each of the profiles.

Organization of This Report

Profiles of different school-affiliated day care programs constitute the bulk of this report.

However, an overview of the status and future direction of the "public school question" may allow readers to understand better the significance of the individual programs.

Accordingly, this report is divided into several other parts:

II. **The Emergence of the "Public School Question"**
   Describes the context in which discussion of the "public school question" has arisen, and suggests why such discussion is likely to persist.

III. **Major Issues in the Debate**
   Summarizes the major arguments made by both proponents and opponents of public school prime sponsorship.

IV. **Profiles**
   Describes how the systems of school-affiliated day care in five communities developed and how they work. Profile sections include history, administrative structure, financing, personnel, coordination with elementary schools, and parent involvement.

V. **Synthesis of Findings and Recommendations**
   Draws out comparisons implicit in the profiles along major programmatic dimensions and reviews their implications for the development of national day care policy. While recommending against any presumed prime sponsorship, this section also offers some guidelines for utilization of the public schools as a resource for day care programs.

VI. **What Lies Ahead?**
   An elaboration of Part I, this section examines the current politics of day care and suggests why the most significant activities in the near future may be on the local rather than the national level.

The three final sections of the report include information which may be helpful to the reader:

VII.   **Notes:** Appropriate citations for all quoted print materials (Section **IV** has footnotes in the text).

VIII.   **Annotated Bibliography:** A guide to selected publications with direct bearing on the "public school question."

IX.   **Alphabet Soup:** A guide to acronyms used frequently in the report.

II.

The Emergence of the "Public School Question"

> In August of 1974, Senator Walter Mondale and Representative John Brademas introduced the newest version of a comprehensive child care bill entitled Child and Family Services Act of 1975 . . . The bill itself has drawn comparatively little comment; the proposed amendments to the bill put forth by the American Federation of Teachers (AFT) have raised a furor.
>
> Barbara Bowman, Director
> Erikson Institute for Early
> Education[1]

What AFT President Albert Shanker proposed in his Congressional testimony was "presumed prime sponsorship" of any national child care program by the public schools. Or, as he put it in his weekly *New York Times* column on September 8, 1974, "the responsibility for the enlarged program [of day care and early education] should be borne by the public schools."[2]

Drawing heavily on an argument first advanced by Edwin W. Martin, Deputy Commissioner for Education of the Handicapped, Mr. Shanker spelled out the logic of his position: expansion of early childhood services is inevitable; random development of early childhood and day care programs can only lead to continued duplication of service, conflict, and wastefulness; a single service delivery system is essential; the public schools are the only agency capable of administering such a program; and with the declining birthrate, they already have the necessary space.[3]

Responses to the Shanker statement and to the AFT's 1976 elaboration of it—a 123-page "action manual" for local leaders entitled "Putting Early Childhood and Day Care Services Into the Public Schools: The Position of the American Federation of Teachers and an Action Plan for Promoting It"—were indeed furious, as organization after organization in the day care field noted how much better designed the AFT's plan was to serve the needs of unemployed teachers than to benefit the nation's children.

9

Nevertheless, the AFT argument immediately commanded serious attention. A major session at the 1974 conference of the National Association for the Education of Young Children asked, "Who Will Deliver Education to Preschool Children?" The following year, the NAEYC conference addressed the question even more directly, featuring a panel entitled, "Should the Public Schools Control Child Care Services?" At the state level, top-level commissions issued recommendations—sometimes contradictory—regarding the public school role in day care. In 1974, for example, Texas Governor Dolph Briscoe's Interagency Task Force on Youth Care and Rehabilitation recommended that, "Child care service programs . . . be provided through the public school districts of the State at the option of the board of trustees of each school district."[4] Shortly thereafter, the Governor's Office of Early Childhood Development issued a separate report asserting that "a young child's needs cannot be fulfilled simply by a downward extension of the school system." Meanwhile, with the Child and Family Services Act under Congressional consideration, virtually every national organization concerned with the education or well-being of children—including major labor unions, like the American Federation of State, County, and Municipal Employees (AFSCME), the United Auto Workers (UAW), and the American Federation of Labor-Congress of Industrial Organizations (AFL-CIO)—set about developing some sort of position paper or statement on the "public school prime sponsorship question."

Although the Child and Family Services Act never made its way through Congress, the "public school question" continues to generate a steady stream of activity. Hardly a professional meeting now takes place without at least one session devoted to it. The 1977 annual conference of the National Association for Black Child Development, for example, featured a debate entitled, "Should the Public Schools Have Exclusive Prime Sponsorship of Day Care?"; the 1978 annual conference of the National Association for the Education of Young Children will include no less than six separate panels devoted to the prospect of public school involvement in day care.

At the same time, major education organizations like the National Education Association (NEA)—which testified briefly in favor of public school sponsorship at 1975 hearings on the Child and Family Services Act—marshalled data to substantiate their views and to keep their constituencies informed. (In 1977, the National Foundation for the Improvement of Education, the research arm of the NEA, prepared a thorough document entitled, "Child Warfare or Early Childhood Education?" outlining the steps NEA might take to establish a "pro-active" policy in this area.)[5]

In 1975, with the Child and Family Services Act first coming under

Congressional consideration and with the AFT first making its claims for a public school role in day care, it was not hard to explain this level of activity. But in 1978, with no national child care legislation on the Congressional agenda and with the AFT "campaign" at a very low level, one might well ask why the public school-prime sponsorship question continues to command such attention from child care advocates, professional educators, and federal and state policy-makers—and why it is likely to persist.

There are many reasons; consider four:

1. Schools and School Teacher Unions are a Powerful Political Lobby for Child Care.

Perhaps the most compelling reason for the attention given by child care advocates to the public school question is their recognition that the passage of any national child care program will require a formidable lobbying effort, and that the public school sector constitutes a major lobby. Indeed, according to Brookings economist Gilbert Steiner, the AFT and its public education allies constitute the only significant lobby—the only hope—for any child care bill.

In *The Children's Cause,* an incisive and often caustic examination of the politics of child care during the last decade, Steiner says "there is little prospect that [the] circumstances" surrounding Congressional passage of comprehensive child development legislation in 1971 "can be replicated." "Renewal of the child development issue and a national program" will only occur, he says, if "self-interest specifically joins social altruism as a driving force"; i.e., any hopes for future legislation depend on organized labor, specifically the AFT, and the "anxiety of public school teachers to protect their job opportunities by reaching for younger clients to keep the pool full." Reminding child advocacy groups of their limited political power, Steiner comments, "While not all members of the [child advocacy] coalition understand the choice as limited to a public school bill or no bill, that really is the choice."[6]

The AFT claims, of course, that it can put together a lobby of the necessary clout, including, "the combined weight of groups that care about the public schools like the AFL-CIO, the National School Boards Association, the Chief State School Officers, the National Congress of Parents and Teachers, the American Association of School Administrators, the National Association of State Boards of Education, and even the National Education Association . . . the same groups who marshalled Congressional support to override a Presidential veto of a $7.9 billion education appropriations bill in the fall of 1975, which is no small feat."[7]

But whether the AFT or any one group could actually mount such a lobby for child care—especially for child care in the public schools—is another story. Other powerful unions, such as the UAW and AFSCME—which represents large numbers and which wants prime sponsorship where its members work, in state and local government—are flatly opposed to public school prime sponsorship. As one Senate staffer says, "I don't think the AFT is any more powerful than these groups, and I think enough members of Congress are leery of the public schools because they would institutionalize day care."

In any event, passage of a new bill will probably require a consensus among groups that carry major sway in Congress. But such a consensus will require resolution of prime sponsorship, the key issue in determining what a national program of child care would look like. Unless it is resolved, then, the public school question might, as Susan Hunsinger and Shelley Kessler, then of the Carnegie Council on Children, suggested, "split the coalition of education, labor, civil rights, day care and community groups that so successfully lobbied for the 1971 bill's passage."[8]

2. Schools Represent the Major "Normalizing" Institution for Children in our Society.

One of the most crucial issues for the future of subsidized day care in this country is the extent to which it can be "normalized," i.e., accepted as a service available to all families, regardless of income, and without the stigma that has traditionally associated it with "deviance," "family pathology," and "welfare."

In this regard, the public education system immediately commands attention, for it has been the major normalizing institution for children's programs. As Norton Grubb says, "the previous history of early childhood education in this country supports the contention that incorporation into the public school system is a prerequisite to the universalization of a program."[9]

This is not to say that the schools are still the only possible way of normalizing day care, that they should be, or that they want to be. Indeed, when a special task force appointed by the Massachusetts House Ways and Means Committee to investigate duplication in state services to children recently recommended that, "The responsibility and the annual appropriation for publicly supported day care should be transferred to the public schools over a two year period of time," the schools were not exactly enthusiastic about the idea.[10] As Mr. Lincoln Lynch, President of the Massachusetts Association of Superintendents testified at public hearings, "The state would be out of their gourd to put day care into the public schools. The public schools are not equipped. We don't have the facilities, the faculty, or the training to handle day care. And if the teachers unions ever got ahold of it, the cost would triple. For God's sake, leave it in the hands of the private contractors."

Whatever role they come to play in day care, if any, the historical place of the schools in American society will probably not allow them to be easily ignored in attempts to formulate any kind of national day care policy.

3. Schools Are Increasingly Offering—Or Being Required to Offer— Part-Day Preschool Programs to Young Children and Their Parents.

For several reasons—quite apart from any desire to provide work for unemployed teachers—school responsibility for preschool children on a half-day basis is increasing. Although the national push for early intervention subsided somewhat in the early seventies, it still provides a dominant rationale not only for Head Start programs—30 percent of which now operate out of public schools—but also for a variety of other early learning programs.[11] According to the most recent figures from the National Center for Education Statistics, 2,783,922 preschool children were enrolled in public school-affiliated programs in fall 1977.[12]

Moreover, the late seventies have seen a revival of the notion that the family in America is disintegrating, a notion that is causing many institutions—including the schools—to examine their role vis-a-vis the family. In 1977, for example, University of Massachusetts President Robert Wood cited the "rapid disintegration" of the American family structure essential to child development," and proposed a massive extension of the public education system to reach children between the ages of one and five.[13] And in Minnesota, a pilot program in Child and Family Education, operating out of 13 local elementary schools, is already at work with the overarching goal of helping to strengthen the family.[14]

Last, but not least, the passage in 1976 of federal legislation for the handicapped (PL 94-142) mandates that schools provide educational services for children with special needs starting at age three, and that such children be mainstreamed with "normal" children. According to Edwin W. Martin, "I think the die is pretty well cast that the public schools are going to provide services for the preschool handicapped; but if they don't provide for normal kids, then you have segregated programs." In the absence of state legislation specifically excluding younger children from the public school responsibility, more and more school systems will be required to develop services for younger clientele.

Clearly, these special education programs, as well as the Minnesota pilot project and the variants of Head Start, are designed to operate half-day at most; i.e., they do not attempt in any way to use the public school mechanism to meet the needs of working parents. At present, only 3.2%

of all day care centers receiving federal funds are sponsored by public schools.[15] And, it should be noted, any Congressional enthusiasm for half-day preschool programs in the schools seems well-equalled by cautiousness about full-day efforts. In December 1977, for example, at a very early stage of House consideration of the Comprehensive Welfare Reform bill (HR 9030), Representative Andrew Jacobs, Jr. (D-Indiana) offered an amendment for a three-year, $126,000 pilot project to use empty public school classrooms as a base for preschool programs. As a Jacobs' aide explained, "We feel that using the public schools is economically efficient and could institutionalize the program in a way Head Start doesn't. But we definitely don't consider it day care."

However, should the trend towards public responsibility for preschool expand to any significant extent, it could act as an impetus for public school day care. As Deputy Commissioner Martin puts it, "If we can get people to agree that special education and early education are legitimate public functions, then we can talk about the hours."

4. Schools Represent a Major Resource and a Major Financial Investment For Most Communities.

National politics aside, the relationship between day care and the public schools is compelling simply because in most communities, schools are the most prominent of all institutions dealing with children, commanding a significant portion of municipal and state budgets. With school enrollments declining, more and more communities will be asking what—if anything—to do with their empty space. That is, even in the absence of any federal day care initiatives or of any push by teacher unions to find a new market for their clientele, more and more communities will find themselves at least discussing the possibility of a public school-day care nexus.

None of these reasons suggest that the public schools should have responsibility for day care, or that they are more capable of providing day care than other institutions. They do suggest, however, that future day care policy, planning, and politics will not easily neglect the relationship between day care and the public schools. The "public school question" will not easily disappear.

As economist Norton Grubb and historian Marvin Lazerson have argued, day care is at a critical stage of its development in this country, paralleling in many ways the situation of the schools in the nineteenth century, before they became "systematized and regularized into school systems":

> The same mixture of public and private funding, with public funds supporting the children of the poor, is characteristic of child care now. Debates

over the propriety of public participation, uncertainty over the relative roles of public and private institutions, a fear that public participation will undermine the family along with the insistance that public participation is necessary to shore up the family, a chaotic and unsystematic delivery system—all these are true of child care now as they were of schooling in the early nineteenth century . . . In that sense, child care (like parent education) appears to be at a critical stage in its development: the direction it takes in the next few decades is likely to shape child care as an institution for a long time to come.[13]

III.

Major Issues in the Debate

Virtually every aspect of day care operation has been included, in one way or another, in the debate about public school prime sponsorship.

The purpose of this section is not to resolve the major arguments but to summarize and, I hope, to elucidate them. It will not attempt an exhaustive representation of organizational positions. Rather, by drawing attention to positions taken by major spokespersons in the debate, it will provide a backdrop against which the specific programs profiled in the main section of this report can be considered.

Examples of arguments in favor of public school prime sponsorship draw heavily on AFT publications, simply because the AFT has elaborated this position more fully than have any other organizations.

PURPOSES OF DAY CARE

Discussions of day care are often characterized by disagreement about its purposes, a disagreement well illustrated, perhaps, by the parable of the elephant and the three blind men: one touched the trunk and said it was a snake; one touched the leg and said it was a tree; one touched the body and said it was a wall. Not surprisingly, each was convinced that the others were wrong.

Much like the elephant in the parable, day care is variously described as serving the needs of parents who are working or as serving the needs of children for what ranges from protective care to early education to child development. Though it may well serve all these functions simultaneously, partisans of different positions—who tend to represent separate communities of interest with different histories of involvement in day care—tend to maintain that theirs is the only accurate description.

Underlying the debate about prime sponsorship, then, is a struggle to define the elephant, once and for all: What *is* day care? What is its purpose?

16

The Social Welfare View

According to the social welfare view, which provides the oldest and most well-established rationale for federal funding, day care provides a protective function for a specific population of children—those "at risk" because their parents are working and, therefore, unable to care for them or incapable of doing so. Though its target population is limited, this view emphasizes a broad range of functions for day care—medical services, counseling, etc.—designed to serve the whole family and not just the child.

Opponents of public school prime sponsorship emphasize that most schools are not and don't want to be "family oriented"; as Gwen Morgan has noted, "When Albert Shanker first proposed school control of the Child and Family Services Act, his first suggestion was removing the word "family" from the name of the bill."[1]

Proponents of school sponsorship, on the other hand, are eager to disassociate themselves from the social welfare view, which carries the stigma of providing a "custodial" service for poor people; hence the AFT argues, "As long as public day care continues to be defined as a poverty program geared to work incentives or tied to income levels, it will probably continue in a custodial vein, there being little pressure from the middle class mainstream to upgrade and broaden it."[2]

Opponents of public school prime sponsorship, it should be noted, agree with the need to remove the stigma from day care and to have it broadly acknowledged that day care serves the needs of all families; they feel, however, that use of the public schools is not the only means to this end.

The Early Education View

The early education view allies day care more closely with schools—and with the nursery and kindergarten movements—than it does with social welfare agencies. Determinedly not "custodial"—though often hard pressed to explain what that means—it often emphasizes two very different purposes: either to prepare children (all children) for success in the existing school system, or to help transform the schools from the bottom up.

Proponents of public school sponsorship are wont to adopt both lines of the early education view, arguing that neither school preparation nor school transformation is feasible if day care exists in its own realm apart from the mainstream of public education; hence the AFT says, we cannot "expect early childhood and day care that remains independent and isolated to have a desired impact on the developmental thinking, or lack of it, that now exists in the regular grades of the public schools."[3]

Opponents of public school sponsorship tend to sympathize with the early education view; they are wary, however, that "preparation" will mean rigid conformity to public school practice, and they are skeptical of any possibilities for wholesale school reform. "Nineteenth and twentieth-century preschooling movements criticized existing educational practices and proposed to reform them," says historian Marvin Lazerson. "Current Head Start expectations are of a similar character. These hopes have invariably led to frustrations. Early childhood educators claimed that later schooling thwarted their innovations. Conversely, elementary school teachers have frequently criticized preschooling for failing to inculcate discipline and condoning practices unconducive to learning."[4]

The Child Development View

Emphasizing the needs of the "whole child," the child development view is often easily allied with both the social welfare and early education views of day care. That is, because it subsumes both the "protective" and the "educational" functions, it is not specifically linked to any one institution, such as the schools, or to any one service population, such as children "at risk." Instead, it serves as an umbrella—or catchword—for all programs serving children.

Nevertheless, proponents of the child development view are often critical of both the social welfare and early education rationales. The former, they claim, encourages "mere custodial care," while the latter emphasizes a narrow range of school-related skills at the expense of developing the "whole child." According to the child development view, responsiveness to the "whole child" requires special sensitivity, though there are major disagreements as to how this sensitivity can be acquired; some say through graduate training, some through life experience with children, others say both are necessary.

Not surprisingly, both proponents and opponents of a major public school role in day care usually subscribe to the child development view, endorsing "developmental day care" to serve the needs of children and of all working parents.

ADMINISTRATIVE ABILITY TO DELIVER SERVICES

Advocates of public school control of day care claim that the schools provide the only existing mechanism for providing an orderly day care program of national scope.

In what has come to be known as his "Buddhist garden" speech, for example, Edwin W. Martin has argued that without public school sponsorship, programs for the care and education of young children will continue to evolve, like his "Buddhist garden," in random fashion:

That is, with a reverence for all living things, we allow to grow around our house what will. I can report to you that this approach involves a minimum of prior planning, that the results are judged to be uneven at best by third-party evaluators, and that later revisions are costly and difficult . . . [In day care] such a development process will result in all of the problems we now see in many of our governmental programs: conflicting responsibilities and assumptions, duplication and overlap, gaps and unevenness of access, wide variations in qualities of service, etc.[5]

Or as the AFT puts it:

At present, federal day care amounts to an organized confusion of competing systems that will never be able to provide comprehensive service no matter how much coordination is attempted. A single, democratically-controlled structural entity should be given the responsibility of administering new day care and early childhood services if there is ever to be a program that will meet national needs. The only structure available to do that job is the public school system. . . . Public education presumed prime sponsorship offers an orderly yet flexible way out of the present chaos of federal child care programs.[6]

Opponents of public school prime sponsorship are often quite ready to agree with both the AFT and Commissioner Martin that there are major problems of coordination under the present system of day care. But they are hardly ready to agree that the schools are the best or even the only agency capable of bringing order out of chaos. Indeed, as they examine public education in communities throughout the country, they point up what Barbara Bowman, former Director of the Erikson Institute, has called "crises of confidence":

By this, I refer to the fact that in many communities the school is failing. One has only to pass the boarded up windows, read the statistics on teacher attacks, and check out achievement scores to be aware that all is not well in many of our public schools . . . This should not be taken to mean that public schools always do an inadequate job working with poor and minority people . . . But poor and minority communities cannot afford to trust the benevolence of any one institution. They cannot trust that they will receive the necessary education from the public schools to thrust them out of the morass of racism, victimization, and paternalism . . . Schools may not be relied upon by the poor and minorities to deliver needed services to their *young children* in any more creditable fashion than they have delivered services to their older children. We must not put all of our early childhood eggs in the same basket.[7]

Similar arguments about the "crisis of confidence" in the schools are made by leading advocacy groups, such as the National Black Child Development Institute, and by groups that usually take quite different stands on most issues, such as the Children's Defense Fund and the National Association for Child Development in Education, the lobby of private-for-profit day care centers. According to NACDE president Wayne Smith, "Society in general considers that its public schools provide a dubious product at dreadful prices." The Defense Fund's director, Marian Wright Edelman, has opposed, "giving schools a whole new set of responsibilities when they are so far from meeting the ones they already have."[8]

Moreover, argue some opponents, the shortcomings of the current system hardly justify the creation of a whole new one. "It would be a mistake," says AFSCME, "to fall into the trap of accepting the argument that because existing child care delivery systems and programs have inadequacies, other mechanisms and institutions, such as the schools, would do a better job. Any new delivery system will have some problems . . . Any new child care program should support and build an existing child care delivery system rather than set up a conflicting system or create the potential for destroying or crippling them."

Since "most public child care funds presently are administered by state and local governments," AFSCME argues that state and local units of government—whose employees happen to be the union's constituency—"are the most logical prime sponsors."[9]

Opponents of public school prime sponsorship (except for NACDE) rarely say that they don't want the schools involved at all in day care; only that the schools should not have exclusive control, that they should not be *presumed capable* of delivering day care services when there is so much indication that they are having difficulty delivering regular elementary education.

In defense of presumed prime sponsorship, the AFT argues that schools would not have to be the sponsor if they were unable or unwilling to in any given community. However, there might well be considerable disagreement in many communities as to whether or not the schools were "able." Under the AFT plan the decision about ability would be made by the schools themselves, with the citizenry expressing its opinions via locally elected Boards of Education.

FLEXIBILITY VS. RIGIDITY

Closely related to arguments about administrative capacity are those about the degree of programmatic flexibility or rigidity that would obtain under different prime sponsors.

At present, day care programs display considerable diversity in both content and format. Would public school prime sponsorship continue to support the current widespread use of family day care homes? How would it affect, if at all, the variety of curriculum emphases? And how willingly would the schools extend to full-year and full-day operation to accommodate parental needs?

Proponents of public school control point to the diversity of educational curricula sponsored across and within school systems. There is no reason, contends the AFT, "why public education agencies, as presumed prime sponsors, could not contract with existing non-profit day care centers" or with family day care providers "to continue their services."[10] Rather than threatening diversity, goes the argument, school sponsorship would simply create an umbrella organization, enabling fiscal and quality control, and facilitating "an orderly yet flexible way out of the present chaos of federal child care programs."[11]

Not all agree, however, that flexibility and the tolerance of variety are hallmarks of the public education system. Indeed, Barbara Bowman cites the—

> . . . inflexibility and rigidity that afflicts large administrative units including public schools. The centralized bureaucracies have considerable difficulty in responding to diverse needs, to changing conditions, and to new visions for the future. Although we have many individual examples of the creativity and innovation that is possible within the public school system, we also have considerable evidence that the large systems are beset with problems of wages and hours, role definitions, standardized treatments, etc. These bureaucratic concerns all too frequently add up to constriction and complacency.[12]

According to Norton Grubb and Marvin Lazerson, "We can expect that child care within the public school system will be increasingly used to prepare children for the elementary grades . . . Location within the public schools explicitly raises the question of purpose, and there is little doubt that those of elementary schools—rather than those of present day care advocates—would come to dominate."[13]

The fact is, of course, that possibilities for constriction and rigidity exist in any system. As Ted Taylor, former Executive Director of the Day Care and Child Development Council of America has said, there is a tendency for any program to become monolithic, "whether it's Head Start, Title IV, day care, or education."[14]

Opponents of public school prime sponsorship seem to agree on this point, arguing not against a public school role, but, as Barbara Bowman has stated, against putting prime sponsorship "in the hands of any one service delivering agency." Bowman suggests the allocation of funds "through a state agency whose primary responsibility is not the direct delivery of child care and education."[15] AFSCME recommends the use of state and local governments, "to stimulate the development of a wide variety of innovative child care programs and arrangements, including community-based centers and union-sponsored centers at the work site."[16] Susan Hunsinger and Shelley Kessler, both formerly of the Carnegie Council on Children, recommend maximizing diversity and flexibility by relying on a new structure of independent citizens councils.[17]

COSTS

According to proponents of public school prime sponsorship, the use of empty classrooms and reliance on one administrative agency would produce significant cost-efficiencies in the delivery of day care services.

With a declining enrollment of some 350,000 students per year projected to continue throughout the decade, says the AFT, "saving could be achieved by utilizing, with appropriate remodeling, this vacant classroom space. The magnitude of this kind of savings, though difficult to estimate, could range between 5 and 10 percent of total cost estimates."[18] And, says the union, noting that "over 60 federal agencies and between 30 and 40 state and local agencies" now have an administrative hand in day care, "Single system delivery would mean putting most of the money into the programs themselves where it can do the most good."[19]

However sensible, say opponents, the claim about facilities may have limited applicability. In communities without any other available space, remodeling classrooms may well be far less expensive than building anew. But in many instances, local licensing codes might make renovation of classrooms equally expensive as, or more expensive than, renovation of existing church, industrial, or recreational facilities. Moreover, some communities might find it more attractive to build an expanded program around family day care homes, the most predominant type of day care today, and one that requires relatively little, if any, remodeling of facilities.

As for the realization of savings through single-system administration, there is little disagreement that the current system could be managed more efficiently. It is not at all clear, however, that the public education system offers the best model for ensuring that dollars go for direct services instead of administration. AFSCME, for example, argues that it would be more cost-effective to build on the existing structure of state and local government control of day care: "It makes little, if any, sense to create a second delivery system in that kind of situation where a fully developed structure already exists, which can easily expand its services."[20]

Even with the realization of savings through administrative streamlining and use of available classrooms, however, it would be misleading to suggest that a public school day care system would save costs overall. If day care teachers shift to the public school salary scale, their salaries—

which everyone agrees are abominably low—will go up substantially, in many instances doubling or tripling. Indeed, one of the arguments being used by the AFT in its "campaign" to recruit the early childhood sector is that all teachers should be paid on the public school scale. Since salaries usually represent 60-75 percent of any day care budget, it follows that the cost of such day care programs would escalate considerably. (This is not to suggest that day care teachers don't deserve or shouldn't be paid on the public school scale; it is, however, to urge that we look realistically at costs.)

Just how much day care operated as part of the public school system would cost the nation is unclear. The Congressional Budget Office has figured the cost of a universally available preschool program used by 75 percent of all three- and four-year-olds in the country at roughly $5.2 billion in 1977. (This includes a 50% federal share of $2.6 billion, along with $2.6 billion from other sources.)[21] But this is not day care, so figures would have to be adjusted upwards to account for operation on the calendar year instead of the school year, and for average operation of 10 hours—as opposed to three hours—per day. The best available projections by economists take the costs of a universally available and utilized day care program up to $30 billion or so per year; but this is without using a public school salary scale, which at current rates would at least double the cost.[22]

Even without sufficient data to project costs accurately, it is clear that, in the absence of adequate financing, a more costly system might only exacerbate the inequities in current policies determining eligibility for public day care services. Under the current system, the poor are subsidized fully, the wealthy pay for their own (usually in-home) services, and families in the middle are generally excluded. *Unless public school day care was adequately financed,* rising costs would mean delivery of service to fewer children.

LICENSING, REGULATION, AND EVALUATION

Both proponents and opponents of public school prime sponsorship are willing to agree on at least one fact: the current system of licensing and regulating day care is inadequate and ineffective. They differ considerably, however, as to the steps that should be taken to bring about effective regulation.

The AFT traces the difficulty to a "confusing array of overlapping federal programs [that] makes enforcing any kind of quality standards a virtual impossibility. When this difficulty is added to the all but incomprehensible variation of state programs and local configurations, keeping a quality watch on the day care picture with any accuracy becomes an impossible feat."[23] Monitoring, goes the argument, could be effectively carried out by consolidation of the delivery system via the public schools, a single agency to set uniform standards.

According to Edwin W. Martin, the schools, more than any other institution, have the capability to set and enforce standards: "They have the mechanisms and the rights under state law and others to be in the standard-setting and regulation business, so with the proper guidance and instruction, they can do that, and in terms of running governmental units, that is a big leg up."[24]

While opponents of public school prime sponsorship may agree on the desirability of uniform standard setting in the day care field, they present three major arguments against the public schools as *the* standard setting agency.

1. The schools tend to abuse their power to set standards. According to Ted Taylor, "the standards that they've set have by and large been arbitrary, have been more designed to protect the prerogatives of the staff and the rights of the staff than they were to protect the interests of the children."[25]

2. Standards of quality will vary from community to community. In a policy statement on prime sponsorship, the Greater Minneapolis Day Care Association recognizes "that different communities have different concepts of quality," and therefore, "strongly suggest[s] that the prime sponsor develop formalized local input (e.g., task forces, area committees, etc.) to help determine quality and technical requirements."[26] In some communities, the public school might be the appropriate agency to develop such input; in other cases, it might not. Therefore, presuming public school prime sponsorship would limit the abilities of some communities effectively to set standards for and regulate their programs.

3. No agency that delivers service should be playing the regulatory or monitoring function as well. This point has been made by Barbara Bowman, AFSCME, and others; none of these critics would exclude the public schools from providing day care services, but all would exclude them from the prime sponsorship role.

PERSONNEL: CERTIFICATION AND QUALIFICATIONS

Of all the issues in the debate about prime sponsorship, none is quite so inflammatory as that of personnel, which cuts through abstract talk about "delivery systems" and gets to the level where most day care and school teachers live—in the classroom. Since it is at the heart of professional self-interest to make the claim for unique abilities to care for children, talk of personnel "personalizes" the debate.

Proponents of public school prime sponsorship, led by the professional organizations and unions, make several major arguments:

1. Current standards for preschool and day care are, at best, inadequate and, at worst, harmful to children. Noting the wide variation in state certification requirements, the AFT concludes: "It is simply inexcusable that many states now require that day care specialists have only a high school education or in some cases even less—that they be 'equipped for work required.' "[27]

2. Uniform certification, best achieved via the public schools, is the only way to guarantee "quality" child care. According to the AFT, "By assuring that teachers are prepared in all aspects of child development and certified on that basis, we may have hope of seeing an end to the more than one century reign of custodial child care in the United States."[28]

3. Public school teachers, more than any other group in society, are qualified to meet the needs of young children. James A. Harris, then president of the NEA, made this point in commenting on the Child and Family Services Act of 1975: "As public school teachers we have the training and the experience to recognize that many of the most important influences on a child and his or her formal learning ability emanate from the very early years. Also by virtue of training and experience we are probably better qualified to determine the shape of those influences than any other definable class."[29]

4. While it may be true that teaching preschoolers is different from teaching tenth graders—or even third graders—public school personnel can be trained or re-trained to meet the special needs of young children.

5. The education system is "in place" for training. According to Edwin W. Martin, "Colleges of education have, with colleges of child development and home economics, joint programming. You can find these programs in a variety of different areas. But there is at the present time a capacity in colleges of education."[30]

By and large, opponents of public school prime sponsorship do not dispute the capability or efficiency of the public education system to certify personnel. However, they do argue on many counts that it is the *wrong* system, providing few if any benefits to children and excluding many of the best teachers from children's lives:

1. Public school teacher certification is no guarantee of quality, and public school teachers, as a group, are no more qualified than non-professionals to teach young children.

At the same hearings at which NEA's Harris commented, Children's Defense Fund director Marian Wright Edelman testified that "Child care work is a separate distinct profession . . . It needs men and women with warmth, openness, and demonstrated effectiveness in dealing with young children. Academic credentials, by themselves, do not measure those kinds of skills."[31]

Barbara Bowman, whose work at the Erikson Institute emphasized training teachers of young children, agrees: "We have little or no evidence to support [the] position . . . that the certified teacher is better able to plan and implement programs for young children. . . . Most certified elementary teachers are paraprofessionals in early childhood education. They must learn to work with the young child and they must learn to work with the child's parents. It is necessary to retrain public school teachers just as it is necessary to train the noncertified teacher."[32] (Such retraining would further add to the costs of a public school day care.)

2. Public school certification tends to discriminate against and to exclude minorities. As the Greater Minneapolis Day Care Association asserts in its position paper on prime sponsorship, "Because systems of professional qualifications have often worked to the exclusion of minority and community people, GMDCA supports maintaining alternative avenues of certification, including competency-based certification."[33] Many other groups also support competency-based criteria and cite the Child Development Associate (CDA) degree, sponsored by the Administration for Children, Youth, and Families, and now being considered for adoption by several states. (The AFT has expressed its opposition to CDA.)

3. Even when minorities are included—largely as paraprofessionals—they tend to be segregated within the system. "I see more and more tendency," says Ted Taylor, "to restrict what a paraprofessional can do in the public school context, and narrowly define the job to make the teacher different from the paraprofessional, to create an order of task and separate people who may very well be equally competent in their capacities to work with children. That's the kind of rigidity that the school systems, it seems to me, very possibly may generate and have generated in many systems."[34]

4. Efforts at public school control have nothing to do with the quality of teaching, and everything to do with providing jobs for unemployed teachers. The coincidence between the interest of teacher organizations in "upgrading" the quality of child care through certification and the rising rate of teacher unemployment is hardly a secret. Under the AFT plan, for example, "career ladder programs" would be implemented to train *all* potential personnel—"unemployed teachers, child care workers, community people, and others." However, "First priority in hiring preschool teachers should be given to former school district employees who have been laid off but have met the requirements for these positions."[35] According to Joyce Black and Marjorie Grossett of the Day Care Council of New York, it is a "moral outrage that the education establishment seeks to solve its problem of empty classrooms and teacher unemployment by enrolling preschoolers in a system unable to meet their needs while refusing to acknowledge its obligation to older children."[36]

5. In giving jobs to middle class teachers, public school day care would drain important economic resources from the communities where poor children live, the communities that have far more effect on their lives than the schools. According to Barbara Bowman, "We have some suggestions from a number of Head Start and other intervention models that poverty's children achieve better in communities steadied by jobs and training in child development. That is, long-term changes in the lives of children are more reliably attained when we can change the lives of their parents and the meaningful others in their communities."[37]

Underlying all the arguments about personnel lie fundamental questions about the future of child care in this country: In any expanded national program, who will do the child caring? What standards, if any, will be set? Who will set them? And with what consequences?

At present, it is difficult to deal in any reasonable way with arguments for or against the qualifications—or potential qualifications—of public school teachers in dealing with young children. There is no reliable data available to indicate whether public school teachers are any better or less able to teach preschoolers, and it is probably true that there is a wide range of variation and individual flexibility within any one group. However, preliminary findings from the National Day Care Study, conducted by Abt Associates, Inc. for the Administration for Children, Youth, and Families, suggest that specialized training appropriate to young children is a more salient ingredient of caregiver quality than years of formal education. That is, though the formal education required of public school teachers might give them the appropriate skills, such education will not be either necessary or sufficient: a different set of standards might well be in order for day care.[38]

For all the cry about credentialing and quality, there also may be considerable flexibility in the requirements set by public schools (or other agencies) when the costs of hiring credentialed personnel become too high. In Nicholtown, South Carolina, to cite one example, public school day care programs require that all teachers have certification in early childhood or elementary education. However, during school vacations and summers, the programs do not use teachers; instead they rely on paraprofessional staff, temporarily elevating their aides to the position of lead teacher. While it is true that enrollment drops off by some 50 percent during these periods, and while the schools do employ a roving Educational Supervisor for a full year, it is hard to argue, on the one hand, that children need credentialed teachers, and on the other, that they only need them during the official school year.

This is an example of fitting children's needs (supposed needs) to the convenience of the school year and administrative structure; put another way, it assumes implicitly that children learn when school is in session (when they need credentialed teachers) and that they do something else when school is not officially in session (when they can have other sorts of teachers).

From the school district's point of view, of course, the fact is that credentialed teachers cost more, and that if day care programs are going to operate out of the schools, there has to be some leeway in personnel policies, allowing for cost savings. Atlanta's school-based program, profiled in this report, has run into this situation head-on and is now reducing its requirements for day care teachers. Initially priding itself on a highly credentialed staff—29 of 33 teachers had the M.A. or equivalent degrees—Atlanta's program will now require, as of July 1, 1979, that head teachers have two years of post-high school training in early childhood education, either at community college or vocational school.

PARENT INVOLVEMENT

Both proponents and opponents of public school prime sponsorship would agree with Marian Wright Edelman that, "The involvement of parents is critical to the success of child care programs."[39] However, there is little agreement about what parent involvement means in practical terms.

Advocates of public school prime sponsorship usually suggest three types of involvement—use of the existing school board mechanism, advisory councils, and parent education. "The school board," according to the AFT, "offers the best means of total community representation in setting policy for children's services, where the community is informed on how to effectively use this process."[40]

Just how representative school boards really are is usually debatable. Recognizing this, the AFT goes on to suggest, "special advisory councils of early childhood and day care parents that will keep them closely informed of the needs and operation of programs."[41] Similarly, Minnesota State Senator Jerome Hughes, proposing a state system of child and family education programs operated from the schools, has recommended the establishment of local elementary attendance area advisory councils "to make it possible for parents to be involved in making policy."[42]

Such special arrangements are no more reassuring to opponents of public school prime sponsorship than the more traditional representation guaranteed by "democratically elected" school boards. Speaking for the child care employees it represents in San Francisco's bilingual programs for Oriental children, AFSCME notes "They have expressed to us their strong fears that there would be less likelihood of such programs being funded under local prime sponsorship than under the present state sponsorship arrangement. They have not seen any evidence of local schools being responsive to either community needs or parent involvement."[43]

The point is echoed again and again by community groups. According to the Greater Minneapolis Day Care Association, "Until the school system can show meaningful parent participation in the decision-making process there will be objections to any control by the school system."[44] Or, as Susan Hunsinger and Shelley Kessler put it in Congressional testimony on the Child and Family Services Act, "It is not enough for parents to sit on 'advisory boards' where they may comment but have no decision making powers nor is it enough to have only the all-or-nothing 'control' of withdrawing their child if dissatisfied."[45]

For Hunsinger and Kessler and for many other opponents of exclusive public school prime sponsorship, meaningful involvement necessitates the inclusion of parents in the decision-making process about policy development and program operation, *including* budget control, staff hiring, and curriculum design, all functions usually delegated to school administrators by their Boards of Education.

Historical precedent suggests, however, that it is unlikely for school administrations to transfer such responsibility to parents. After reviewing the history of day care in America, and the experience of the California Children's Centers in particular, Norton Grubb and Marvin Lazerson conclude, "As limited as parental involvement is [In the Children's Centers], it nonetheless is more than exists in elementary and secondary schools. All the evidence on bureaucratic functioning, professionalization, and the current practices of public education indicates that parents will lose control of day care if public schools gain control."[46] To prevent such an occurrence, Grubb and Lazerson recommend that in any federal child care programs, "parental control should be legislated."[47]

While it may be true that public school bureaucracies restrict parent control, it would be erroneous to conclude that such control exists in most non-public school-related day care programs. For unless parents have clear and full responsibility for the two critical tasks of hiring staff and budgeting (as they do in the Brookline Extended Day program), then regardless of the auspices (be they private nonprofit, public school, or parent co-op) and regardless of nominal or formal structures for involvement (such as Parent Advisory Councils, Boards of Directors, etc.), parent input varies enormously from program to program. Often such variation depends greatly on the personalities and mix of people—such as the center director, board president, and head of the parent group. It also varies with program crises; loss of a key staff member or imminent loss of Title XX or other funds has been known to produce high level, though temporary, parent involvement.

It is also unclear that all or even most working parents—given their time constraints—want control of budgeting, hiring, and other matters, or that they feel uninvolved or disenfranchised unless they are responsible for these matters. Of course, some parents do want such responsibility, and some programs have been very effective with this sort of involvement (the Brookline Extended Day Program, which operates in conjunction with a public school system, is a good example). But some parents also feel they have satisfactory, if not optimal, involvement and influence in decision-making when informal avenues to communication exist, as opposed to formal structures. This is true of public school and non-public school programs.

In sum, parent involvement is often a more complex and delicate matter than has been suggested so far in the debate about prime sponsorship. Though public school auspices might restrict parental involvement, there is no guarantee that other auspices will necessarily involve them any more unless parent responsibilities are clearly structured into the program. But mandating parent control—the only sure way to guarantee involvement—will not necessarily meet the needs or preferences of most parents. The difficult issue of structuring realistic and meaningful parent involvement will be taken up again in light of our examination of programs in five different communities.

IV.

Profiles

Oakland Children's Centers, Oakland, California

SYNOPSIS

The Oakland Children's Centers comprise the oldest and one of the largest of school district-operated day care programs in the country. The program now serves some 2,200 children from infancy to 14 years of age, using 20 facilities adjacent to elementary school buildings and four facilities located on community college campuses. But it is not just longevity or scope that makes the Children's Centers important for this report: in 1974 the Oakland Unified School District agreed to give its credentialed Children's Centers teachers the same salary and the same 180-day work year as other public school teachers. While Oakland's "parity" policy improved the working conditions of some day care teachers, it simultaneously strained the ability of centers to maintain continuity of children's caregivers, and raised important questions about the future of public school-based day care in other cities throughout the country.

SERVICE DATA

Type and Number of
    Programs: 24 Children's Centers, including:

4 Community College Centers serving infants and preschoolers (up to four years, nine months)

20 centers serving preschool (2-5) and school-aged children; 16 of these 20 are adjacent to elementary schools, and the other four will be by 1978.

Type and Number of Programs: (*Cont.*)	3 of these 20 are "ethnic centers," serving American Indian, Chinese, and Chicano populations.
Hours of Operation:	7 AM-6 PM, year-round; some variation within these limits from center to center.
Children:	2,200 in December 1976; approximately half preschoolers and half school-aged.

Financing: (1976-77)

Title XX:	$3,561,570	(59%)
Local taxes:	$2,361,489	(39%)
Parent Fees:	$ 105,000	(2%)
School District:		(0%)
Total:	$6,028,059	

Costs: (1976-77) $2.10 per child per hour; state maximum reimbursable rate was $1.28 per child per hour

Parent fees are on a sliding scale.

Personnel: All staff are employees of the Oakland Public Schools.

Salaries:
$8,733 - $17, 481 (Credentialed Teachers)
$6,999 - $11,142 (Certificated Teachers)
$3.24 - $5.67/hour (Instructional Assistants) for 3.5 hour day

HISTORY AND DEVELOPMENT

Oakland's Children's Centers comprise one of the largest and oldest school district-operated day care programs in the country. Administered by the Oakland Unified School District under the auspices of the State Department of Education, the program served some 2,200 children in 1976-77, and was the third largest Children's Center program in the state.*

There was never any question about the appropriateness of public school sponsorship in 1933, the height of the Depression, when the Oakland schools first became involved in the care of young children. When WPA funds were allocated to meet the educational and nutritional needs of preschoolers—and to provide jobs for unemployed teachers—full-day "playschools" were established, as they were in many other school systems, at 19 elementary sites. Unlike most other school systems, however, Oakland has continued its day care, in one form or another, ever since.

The playschools continued operating with WPA support until 1943 when the Lanham Act made federal funds available for day care. The California legislature authorized its State Department of Education to administer programs for the "care and supervision" of children and Oak-

*San Francisco and Los Angeles have larger programs.

land's "playschools" were officially converted to child care centers, serving employed parents for a weekly fee of $3.50.

In California, unlike every other state in the nation, day care did not disappear with war's end and the withdrawal of Lanham Act funds. In 1946, faced with a strong child care lobby and industry's continuing need for female labor, the California legislature voted to share the costs of day care with local school districts for one more year. The state matched local dollars—generated by parent fees—on a two-to-one basis, and school districts like Oakland provided buildings and some administrative services on an in-kind basis. In contrast to current programs, Aid to Families with Dependent Children (AFDC) recipients were ineligible: child care was explicitly for children of working and fee-paying parents.

State appropriations continued on an annual and biennial basis from 1946 to 1957, when the legislature voted to extend subsidy of child care indefinitely—with the level of funding to be determined from year to year. At the same time, the legislature allowed for a new source of day care revenue; to support their programs, local school boards were empowered to levy an "override tax," the same mechanism used in California to generate income for earthquake-proofing of the schools.

In Oakland, interestingly, the first use of the override tax was to buy land to get the day care programs out of their public school buildings, which were often substandard. According to Maxine Christopher, then director of the Children's Centers in Oakland, "We got out primarily because of fire and safety reasons, but we also needed a different set of rules for children; school rules were too restrictive for young children."

Mounting national interest in early childhood education in the mid-1960s brought several major changes to state-supported child care in Oakland and other cities in California. In 1965, an amendment to the California Education Code changed the program's name from "child care" to "Children's Centers" and its goals from "care and supervision" to "provision for supervision and instruction of children." State legislation passed in the same year allowed the use of California dollars to generate federal matching funds for the so-called "disadvantaged," and enabled the Children's Centers program to expand rapidly during the next decade: from 1966-1976 the number of centers in Oakland doubled from 12 to 24, and the number of children served from 1,100 to 2,200.

However, federal dollars brought with them restrictive federal eligibility guidelines. As Norton Grubb and Marvin Lazerson observe, "Almost overnight the centers' clientele changed from working class families who paid substantial fees to families on welfare who paid nothing. . . . Ironically, at precisely the moment that early childhood education was receiving nationwide prominence, the Children's Centers were being increasingly confined to welfare-oriented goals by federal guidelines."*

---

*W. Norton Grubb and Marvin Lazerson, "Child Care, Government Financing, and the Public Schools: Lessons from the California Children's Centers." *School Review*, volume 86, no. 1 (November, 1977), p. 16.

This dramatic shift in the population of day care consumers coincided, in the late 1960's, with equally significant shifts in the status of day care teachers, who, in Oakland, as in almost all other cities throughout the country, worked longer hours and received less pay than their public school colleagues.

"Ever since we've been in existence we've been working towards the same type of benefits and status as other educators," says Maxine Christopher. When she became director of the Children's Centers in 1957, Ms. Christopher saw the credentialing of child care workers as the major route towards such status: "Realistically, I knew any change in salary would be linked to credentials. We were part of a school system, and school systems look at pieces of paper. So I told my teachers it was important to work towards their baccalaureate degrees with an emphasis on child development."

Meanwhile, Ms. Christopher and other leaders in early education pressed for the State Department of Education to develop a credential that would recognize the special skills required of work with young children. By 1968, the state had adopted a credential with specialization in child development, and Children's Centers administrative staff had petitioned the Oakland Board of Education to place Children's Centers teachers—at least those with credentials—on the same salary scale as elementary teachers. Backing the request were Oakland's teacher unions—which were beginning to see child care workers as a possible constituency. "Employees in the centers wanted an updating and upgrading of the program, and we wanted to represent them," says Hal Boyd, Director of the Oakland Education Association, local affiliate of the NEA. "After all, the district had ballyhooed the program around the state as one that did more than babysitting."

While the Board of Education took the request under advisement for one year, the Children's Centers teachers made drastic cutbacks, worked overtime for free, and saved some $90,000 of operating funds. "We showed a year-end surplus," says Ms. Christopher, "saved on the backs of teachers." More persuasive to the Board, however, was "the possibility of using the district override tax for salaries, not just capital outlays, in the future." Beginning with the 1968-69 school year, those Children's Centers teachers with a B.A. plus a fifth year of graduate work were put on the same salary schedule as other public school teachers. There was, however, still one catch: public school teachers worked 180 days per year; Children's Centers teachers worked 255 days, 41 percent more time for "equal" pay.

It took six more years, and some 30 years from their opening, for teachers in Oakland's Children's Centers to become the first in the country to achieve parity with their public school colleagues. Though Children's Centers administrative staff long favored this upgrading, equalization of salary and days worked (180) was finally accomplished through negotiations with Oakland's two major teacher unions—AFT and NEA— each of which claims credit for success in bargaining with the school district. (Of the nine seats on the union bargaining council, seven were held by the Oakland Education Association, the NEA affiliate, and two by the United Teachers of Oakland, the AFT affiliate. OEA clearly controlled the voting on the union side, but UTO claims that it pressured and finally embarrassed OEA into fighting for parity.)

Union battles aside, the fact is that even with its substantial cost increases to the Children's Centers program—about $1 million per year— parity offered distinct advantages to the school district. Above all, it made credentialed Children's Centers and elementary teachers interchangeable, since they now had the same salary and work year. Faced with declining enrollment in its elementary grades, the school district could avoid laying off teachers by transferring them to Children's Centers. And, since the funding sources for the Children's Centers and regular public school program were separate, the school district could make these transfers without incurring any additional operating costs in its regular school budget. (Though several such transfers have occurred, no specific figures were available at the time of this report.)

The effects of parity on the operation of the Children's Centers have been complex. Whether or not parity has given child care teachers the "status of educators" that Ms. Christopher sought, it has certainly made work in the Centers more desirable to elementary school teachers. "Day care has become very attractive," says one administrator of personnel in the Oakland schools, "and it's obvious why. Compared to the schools, the Children's Centers have small sites and an open classroom format. And they don't have to work 180 days between September and June; they can spread long vacations throughout the year. We don't get Children's Centers teachers wanting to go into the public schools anymore. It's the other way around."

However, the willingness of Children's Centers teachers to accept elementary teachers into their programs is, at best, ambivalent. In some instances, parity has exacerbated longstanding rivalries between two professional groups. As one Children's Centers supervisor says, *"They're* trained to teach elementary school. We're trained to meet the needs of young children. If an elementary teacher comes in, she's not worth a damn to me."

Even more significantly, parity has widened the gap between professionals and paraprofessionals within the Children's Centers programs, for in upgrading working conditions for credentialed Children's Centers teachers—i.e., those with a B.A. degree plus a fifth year of education (which can but does not have to be in early childhood)—it has obstructed, if not eliminated, the longstanding career ladder for non-academically oriented staff, often "community people" who held the positions of Teacher's Assistant (TA) and Instructional Assistant (IA). The IA position required a high school diploma or equivalency; advancement to TA or "permit teacher" status came with 60 units of college credit, often achieved with the A.A. degree at a community college. However, the 180-day parity agreement included elimination, by attrition, of the Teacher's Assistant position, and the stipulation that IA's could work no more than half time.

By 1976, with a 41 percent reduction in TA's, the Children's Centers were clearly moving towards a two-tiered system of highly credentialed full-time teachers and minimally credentialed part-time Instructional Assistants, with a large educational gap between the two tiers.* Only by earning the full credential—which takes five years of college course-work—can IA's move up in the system, an implicit devaluation of the skills brought to the Children's Centers in the past by people who have neither the inclination nor the income for schoolwork. As Grubb and Lazerson have observed, this "increases the pressure upon Center teachers to obtain full credentials, and reconfirms the notion that credentialing is related to competence and can stand as a surrogate measure of competence." [†]

To help Children's Center staff earn their credentials, the Oakland public schools have adopted a number of measures, some now written into the negotiated employment package. School district "counselors" evaluate the records of teaching staff and advise them on how to proceed with their academic work. All teaching assistants are allowed to accumulate vacation days so that they can attend school for an entire semester. Moreover, the district has provided facilities late in the afternoon for the offering of college and university courses.

Midst all the efforts to make credentialing easier, however, some head teachers note that resentment of many teachers' assistants has increased: "Lots of them don't want to go to school. Why should they? They do the same work anyway." And noting the limitations of the system, one long-time teacher assistant says, "They don't give the courses at the right times. I'm a 6 o'clock teacher. I can't make it to 4 o'clock or even 6 o'clock classes. I don't even get out until 6 o'clock; and what if someone is late? I know they have a right to upgrade the program, but it doesn't help me a bit."

Reactions are even mixed about the new 180-day work year for fully

---

*No figures are available on the number of TA's who have earned their credential since parity. But in 1970, TA's represented 39 percent of the teaching staff (45 of 116); in 1976, TA's represented 23 percent of the teaching staff (53 of 234).

[†]Grubb and Lazerson, p. 23.

credentialed teachers. It is, of course, highly desirable from the individual teacher's point of view: "Taking time off every two months or so lets you get refreshed, so you're better with the kids." But it has also presented the Children's Centers with a number of operational issues that highlight major distinctions of purpose between child care and public school. For one, the 180-day year strains the efforts of centers to maintain the continuity of caregivers needed so much by young children.

Before "parity" went into effect, children in day care were already dealing with multiple caregivers; after "parity," the number necessarily increased. If all teachers were to take their vacations during the summer, as do public school teachers, there would be a sudden and severe disruption in the experience of the children. But for teachers to alternate their vacation schedules would mean that the entire staff would never be together at any one time, making it difficult to achieve staff cohesiveness, and would necessitate a constant shuffling in and out of substitute teachers, each in need of training. Indeed, the Children's Centers Chinese center, which provides bicultural instruction in Chinese and English, found it so difficult to find substitutes, that it relies on its own staff members to substitute while they are on vacation. "The children and the programs would have been better off," says one experienced teacher, "if the parity agreement allowed us to pro-rate an increment to our salary over the long year. Day care isn't elementary school. But I guess we won what we won on elementary school terms."

In the future, it may well be that any more "gains" are also made in elementary school terms, for the conditions under which Children's Centers teachers work will increasingly be determined by teacher unions. In May 1977, after a year-long legal battle, the California Educational Employment Relations Board (EERB) designated the Oakland Education Association (OEA), the largest of the city's teacher unions, to represent all *credentialed* child care teachers in annual collective bargaining. OEA barely won out over the Child Care Employee's Union (CCEU), an independent local organization that represented both professional and paraprofessional Children's Center staff, and that had argued vehemently for preserving the involvement of "community people" in the Centers and the autonomy of the Centers from the schools.

In awarding rights to representation to the OEA, the EERB unexpectedly adopted a significant part of the CCEU position; it said that child care work was different from public school teaching, and that the OEA would have to represent its child care teachers with a separate bargaining unit. However, this technicality is not likely to affect the OEA thrust, which is to make the conditions of child care teachers even more like those of their public school colleagues. In its 1977 Negotiations Proposal, for example, OEA has requested, among other things: 1) that all teachers work a seven-hour day, including a 50-minute duty-free lunch, a 50-

minute duty-free preparation period, and a 15-minute break; 2) that the work year for teacher assistants be reduced from 241 to 180 days; 3) that the transfer of public school teachers to the Children's Centers be facilitated by providing 15 days of training and three inservice credits to all teachers who transfer, as well as an additional 20 percent in salary to the Children's Centers teacher who does the training.*

Like the long sought "parity," all of these demands would necessitate increased costs to the Children's Centers program, and raise fundamental questions about the future of the public school-day care nexus. Will there be any room for "community people" in a program that adopts public school credentialing as its norm? Who will bear the costs of the salary increases that attend such credentialing? Will the increased costs of operation necessitate a decrease in services to children and families? Will the Board of Education and the taxpayers in Oakland continue to finance the increasing costs of Children's Centers teachers through the local override tax, as they have been doing since 1968? Or will they, as in Atlanta (profiled elsewhere in this report) start to question the need for such an "upgraded" program?

The answers to all these questions—and others—will be tied inextricably not only to local politics but to state and national politics, as well. For although the Children's Centers are now well established, they are largely financed by Title XX and, therefore, subject to ever-shifting currents in federal definitions of what day care is, who is eligible for it, what the appropriate staff-child ratios are, etc. In the absence of any strong position on day care from the President or Congress, it is not clear what direction these currents will take.

It is clear, however, that school administrators throughout California and throughout the nation will be asking the Oakland Public Schools and the Children's Centers the same question they asked Jim Wilson, the schools' chief negotiator, after parity went into effect: "What the hell are you doing?"

ADMINISTRATIVE STRUCTURE

District Level

According to their director at the time of this writing, Mr. Sherman Skaggs, the Children's Centers operate like a "small school district within a school district."

The point is best illustrated, perhaps, by comparison with Atlanta, which has a day care program of comparable size. In Atlanta, public schools are divided into four administrative areas, each with its own

---

*As this report went to press, negotiations had been completed. None of requests was granted, though the new contract specifically continues teachers' rights to a 30-minute duty-free lunch, 30-minute duty-free preparation period, and a 15-minute break.

ADMINISTRATION, OAKLAND

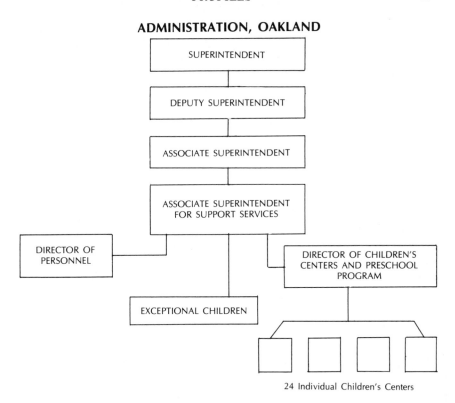

24 Individual Children's Centers

superintendent, who has area-wide responsibility for the implementation of day care and other programs. In Oakland, the administrative lines of responsibility are drawn by program, not by area. As the following chart indicates, the Children's Centers are one of several programs administered centrally within the school district.

Center Level

At the individual program level, Children's Centers are administered by a center supervisor. (Centers vary in size from 25 to 130 children.) Since all are in facilities separate from elementary schools, principals have little of the jurisdiction that they have in cities like Brookline or Atlanta. Although a working relationship between Centers and elementary schools exists in many cases, it is also true, as the Director of Children's Centers says, that "You might go talk to a principal who doesn't have a Children's Center adjacent and she or he might not even know the Children's Centers exist!"

Within the next two years, plans call for at least four new Children's Centers to be integrated architecturally with their local elementary schools, a return more or less to the original design of the WPA "playschools.'' Administrative lines of responsibility for these arrangements have not been drawn yet, and it is not clear how much autonomy the Children's Centers will retain.

FINANCING AND COSTS

Financing

Financing for the Children's Centers during FY 1977 came from several sources, as indicated in the following chart and as explained below:

Title XX:	$3,561,570
Local Taxes:	$2,361,489
Parent Fees:	$ 1,195
School District:	00

• **Title XX.** During the last thirty years, financing of the Children's Centers has shifted substantially from the state to the federal government. From 1946-1951, for example, the state contributed two-thirds of Children's Centers revenue, with the other third coming from parent fees. Since the mid-60's, however, California has increasingly relied on federal Title money, now available largely under Title XX amendments to the Social Security Act, which require a state matching share of 25 percent. At the present time, California contributes $890,393 for operation of the Oakland Children's Centers, generating federal revenues of $2,671,177. The state, then, is now contributing roughly 25 percent of revenues; parents contribute but a fraction of program revenues.

If California's 1977 fiscal policy for non-Children's Centers day care is any indication, the balance of state and federal funding may tilt again. During FY 1977, the state of California began ''buying out'' many of its community-based, Title XX programs; i.e., state dollars were used to replace federal Title XX dollars, which were then diverted to programs other than day care.

In giving up its use of federal dollars for day care, the state also relieved itself of the need to comply with Federal Interagency Day Care Requirements, which specify, among other things, strict staff-child ratios. The state claims that by loosening these ratios—i.e., by having a few more children for each staff member—it can run programs of the same quality and same cost, but for more children. Opponents of the buy-out point out that since very few centers have any space for more children, the state is simply using the buy-out to save money by laying off teachers.

A buy-out of Children's Centers—if it should occur—would shift most funding back to the state.* It is important to note, however, that a buy-out

---

*The four Children's Centers located at community colleges, which operate somewhat apart from the other Children's Centers, have already been bought out.

is largely a fiscal and accounting convenience for the state and would not really diminish Children's Centers dependence on federal funds.

• **Local Taxes.** Since 1957, the Oakland Board of Education has been empowered to levy a school district "override tax" for operation of the Children's Centers. Originally set at six cents per $100 of assessed property value, the override was restricted for use on capital expenditures; by 1977, it had risen to 18.4 cents per $100 and was being used to cover both capital and general operating expenditures, including the increased cost of teachers paid under the parity agreement.

The importance of the tax override to the continuing operation and expansion of the Oakland Children's Centers cannot be overestimated. Even if Title XX or state funds should increase, additional children cannot be served without additional facilities. However, the only source of funds for capital outlay is the local tax override, which is also being used to pay the increasing cost of teacher salaries. In the next few years, Oakland's Board of Education may well face a trade-off between payment of teachers and expansion of services that foreshadows developments in other communities.

• **Parent Fees.** Parent fees, which generate $1194.94, a tiny fraction of program operating costs, are paid on a sliding-fee scale established by the state and geared to adjusted gross income and family size. Individual fees range from five cents per hour to $1 per hour and are collected by center supervisors in each center.

• **School District of Oakland.** The school district does not contribute any monies from its general operating budget. Conversely, no Children's Centers funds may be used for operation of the public school program.

Costs

Cost per child for separate program components is not available; average cost per child was $2.10 per hour. Administrative costs represented one percent of the 1976-77 resources budget; instructional costs represented 60 percent.

ELIGIBILITY

Eligibility is in accord with Title XX guidelines developed at the state level.

Children are eligible if they are between ages 2 and 14, and if their parents were employed, participating in a work-training program, or attending school. (Children as young as six months can attend three of the community college-based Centers.)

There are 2,000 children in the program; of those, seven percent are not eligible for Title XX. Their fee varies with income according to a state fee schedule.

Priority is given to single-parent families that are current, former, or potential AFDC recipients; highest priority goes to single parent current recipients who are participating in federal or state vocational training programs.

However, special provision to treat two-parent families equally with one-parent families has been made at one particular center, the Centro Infantil, because of the large number of low-income two-parent working families in the Mexican-American community it serves.

A state buy-out of Title XX funds for the Children's Centers, should it occur, would change eligibility criteria to reflect an increased percentage of children from fee-paying families.

PERSONNEL

All Children's Centers staff are employees of the Oakland Public Schools.

There are three major levels of staff responsibility within the Children's Centers: 1) administration and supervision of each center is done by a center supervisor (most centers also have an assistant center supervisor—the best analogy is principal and vice principal); 2) classroom teaching and planning are done by credentialed and certificated teachers; and 3) "helping" with classroom teaching is done by instructional assistants. While it is often difficult to differentiate in practice between credentialed and certificated teachers, there are substantial differences in the criteria required and the salaries paid for each of these positions.

Criteria

The minimum qualification for teachers, center supervisors, and assistant center supervisors is a California teaching credential, which requires, in addition to the B.A. degree, a fifth year of study in early childhood education, elementary education, or "multiple subjects," i.e., reading, mathematics, etc.

The Oakland Children's Centers give preference to candidates with the early childhood credential. Implemented in 1968, the credential requirement puts a premium on academic, as opposed to experiential, learning, and inherently favors those able to attend five years of college.

"We won't even interview prospective teachers now unless they have a credential," says Mr. Sherman Skaggs. Under this system, the application of a credentialed graduate of the state university system with little or no experience would automatically take precedence over that of a certificated (i.e., non-credentialed) person with ten years of working experience in the Children's Centers. "You miss some good people," says Mr.

Skaggs, "but you solve that problem by saying that if you interview people you should be able to come up with somebody comparable.

Children's Centers teachers who do not have their credentials fall into two categories: certificated teachers and instructional assistants. Certificated teachers, also called "permit teachers," are required to have either a regular or provisional Children's Centers permit. The regular permit requires a B.A. with a major in child development or early childhood education, or sixteen related semester hours of study. The provisional permit, held by many staff members, requires 60 hours of college coursework and evidence of continuing progress towards a B.A. degree. Instructional assistants are not required to have any education beyond a high school degree; evidence of some working experience with children is desirable but not necessary.

Salaries

In comparing salaries within the Children's Centers, it is especially important to note that credentials determine not only salary but amount of time worked during the year. Credentialed teachers work a 180-day year, comparable to their public school colleagues; permit and provisional permit teachers work a 220-day year.

Children's Center salaries are, in effect, on three scales. Credentialed teachers are on the scale used for other public school teachers. Certificated teachers have a separate schedule printed on the same document as the credentialed teacher salary schedule. Before parity, certificated teacher (teacher assistant) salary was approximately 80 percent that of credentialed teachers; taking the difference between the 180-day and 220-day year into account, certificated teachers now make closer to 60 percent. Instructional assistants are on a "paraprofessional" scale also used for IA's in elementary school classrooms.

Salary ranges are as follows:

Center Supervisors:	same as credentialed teachers plus $1,701/year.
Assistant Center Supervisor:	same as credentialed teachers plus $1,020/year.
Credentialed Teachers:	$8,733-$17,481/year.
Certificated Teachers:	$6,999-$11,142/year.
Instructional Assistants:	$3.24-$5.67/hour for an average of 3.5 hours per day.

Hiring Procedures

Hiring of all teaching staff is done at the central administrative level, and not by individual centers. In all cases, however, hiring procedures allow for input by parent and teacher representatives from centers; in some cases, as will be explained, personnel decisions are made *de facto* by the parent board and not by the central administrative staff.

Unlike Atlanta, Oakland does not allow the "bumping" of Children's Center staff by public school staff with seniority. However, priority for all vacant Children's Center positions has to be given to extra contracted teachers who have the early childhood, elementary, or multiple subjects credential.

"If we don't want them," says one administrator, "We have to come up with a rationale for why they don't fit. For example, the applicant doesn't exhibit any experience working in an open setting, or the applicant has questionable skills in relating to small children." With declining enrollment in the elementary schools, Children's Centers staff may be increasingly pressed to consider the qualifications of their elementary school colleagues.

Applications are received by the Personnel Office of the Oakland Public Schools, screened for eligibility, and then referred to the Children's Centers office. A Children's Centers team consisting of central administrative staff and a center supervisor from the center with a vacancy then select potential candidates, interview them, and make three recommendations to the Director of the Children's Centers.

Parental involvement in this process varies, depending on individual centers. In all cases, parents can sit in with center supervisors and central administrative staff as members of the screening and interviewing team. However, their recommendations do not necessarily determine the choice of candidates.

In some cases, parents have asserted their "rights" to influence the hiring process. This has been especially true of Oakland's bilingual centers, the most recent additions to the Children's Centers program. During one recent hiring, for example, 13 parents and three staff members showed up to be included on the interviewing team. Parents at the Centro Infantil leave the central administration little room to select its staff; they monitor the entire hiring process, and then recommend only one acceptable candidate to the Director of the Children's Centers.

Explaining why these groups have been so active, one Children's Centers administrator says, "These groups haven't had services for a long time. Now they want to make sure they get the services they need. And at all the bilingual centers the staff has a strong commitment to parent involvement; they come from the same community; they live and work with them in other areas of life."

COORDINATION WITH ELEMENTARY SCHOOL

Though not yet accomplished, the development of a coordinated curriculum between the Children's Centers and the elementary schools in Oakland is being talked about. However, coordination means different things to different people. As an administrative matter, coordination seems generally desirable; as one fourth grade teacher says, "I think continuity and consistency is important." However, there is little agreement about the underlying educational goals of coordination, about whether the curriculum of the Centers or the public schools should be the leading edge for change.

Under the leadership of its new superintendent, Dr. Ruth Love, the Oakland Public Schools, like many school systems throughout the country, are moving "back to basics" and towards "competency-based curricula." An Instructional Strategy Council has been formed to make recommendations about "improving student achievement." One of its 1976 policy statements calls for the "active participation of the Children's Centers . . . in the development of a comprehensive, performance-based curriculum for the Oakland School District."

Meanwhile, a Children's Centers task force has developed its own Integrated-Developmental Curriculum which outlines an approach to dealing with the "whole child," and which stands in antithesis to any performance-based approaches. According to the coordinator of curriculum development, "We did it in part as a basic document for all staff, an attempt to define and describe the philosophy and principles which underlie the operation of the Children's Centers. And we did it in part as a guide for the large number of elementary teachers who are moving into the Children's Center program."

"I believe the benefits would be greater to the elementary schools than to the Children's Centers," says one union leader. "Perhaps some of what's going on at the Children's Centers would rub off. There are just too many kindergarten classrooms where the children all sit down and do the same ditto—and these are five year olds.. . . Though there are some Children's Centers where that's true too."

As of yet, there have been no widespread efforts—as there have been in Atlanta, for example—to coordinate day care and elementary curricula. Actual links between the Children's Centers and elementary schools vary considerably and usually depend upon the relationship between the school principal and the Center's Supervisor.

At the Jefferson Center, for example, the center supervisor of some fifteen years meets formally with the principal "once a week about the community concerns that affect all of us. . . . And I'm up there about twice a week for other matters. I even have a mailbox up there." At the beginning of each year, her teachers meet with the elementary school staff to share objectives; public school teachers visit the Center to see where their charges spend a good part of their day; and Children's Centers teachers often receive calls asking if they will help a particular child with homework.

Some centers even require that school-aged children do homework or homework-related material during at least some of the time before and after school. (With elementary classes beginning at 9 or 10 AM in some cases, there are often long stretches before school for homework.)

Highly articulated coordination is probably the exception rather than the rule. As the center supervisor at another center says, "We have a very loose arrangement. There are no joint efforts, but we know more or less what their curriculum is from the report cards. Unfortunately, most of our contact is a result of a child who has a problem."

According to another teacher, "I think we could do a lot more reinforcement educationally if we knew what was going on. A lot of it now is by clue, guessing, from seeing their papers and having a general idea of what they're supposed to be doing. There are a lot of things we could teach here; we have the time. But I think there are a lot of mistaken ideas in the schools about what we're doing; if the schools understood better what we're doing, we could help them. It's really nobody's fault, though. It's the system. The problem is when she [the classroom teacher] doesn't have them, I do; and when I don't have them, she does."

Efforts to bring classroom teachers together with Children's Center teachers will soon be facilitated in at least two schools, where renovations call for Children's Centers to be located in the school building, as they were some thirty years ago. But just what efforts the total school system will make at coordination—and whether the dominating influence will be "back to basics" or the "integrated-developmental curriculum" or something else—is unclear.

PARENT INVOLVEMENT

Formal opportunities for parent involvement exist at the center level, through the Parent Advisory Board, and at the district level, through the District Advisory Committee, which includes representatives from each of the centers.

Functions of the Parent Advisory Board vary considerably from center to center, and are regulated less by any official guidelines than by the relationship established between parents and center supervisors. Parent Boards are supposed to meet on a monthly basis; some meet less frequently but involve parents other ways—as classroom aides, or to help raise money and accompany children on excursions.

Involvement of parents is especially high at the bilingual, bicultural centers. As the supervisor of the Chinese center explains, "I think this is the only agency in Oakland that Asian parents can relate to. Even if their languages are different, they share a lot of the same customs and foods."

At the Centro Infantil, all parents are strongly encouraged to attend the monthly meeting. "If they don't come, though," says center supervisor Bertha Canton, "there are other alternatives for contributing." Although it is not official Children's Centers policy, the parent board at the Centro asks that parents who cannot attend meetings volunteer three hours during the next week or contribute $10 to a private parent fund used for program enrichment.

Though there are no formal Children's Centers provisions for a parental role in the selection of staff or the development of curriculum, this also varies from center to center. At the Centro Infantil, for example, parents do both, supplementing (and perhaps supplanting) central administrative staff of the Children's Centers. A committee of eight parents screens all applications, solicits a written essay, and then interviews all finalists. The full parent body then makes one—and only one—recommendation to the Children's Centers staff.

Attempts by a small group of parents to gain similar control at the District level have not been as successful. In Fall 1976, members of the District Advisory Committee petitioned the Superintendent of Schools for a greater role in determining Children's Centers policy. "We felt we were a token committee," says Marlyn Murray, one of the parents. "We weren't really involved as part of the decision-making process for the Children's Centers." Among this group's demands were: parent representation in the hiring of any staff who work with children, in budget setting, in needs assessment, and in teacher evaluation; publication of a newsletter for parents; and reinstatement of a parent coordinator position, which had been eliminated in the previous year.

Following these requests, Oakland's Superintendent of Schools appointed a Task Force to review the Children's Centers program. The Task Force, including some parent representatives, affirmed the reinstatement of the parent coordinator position, and recommended review by parent boards of individual center budgets; however, in personnel matters it strongly held that the parental role was to advise, not to select.

MONITORING AND EVALUATION

Monitoring and evaluation of the Children's Centers is done at several levels.

Some individual centers—in some cases individual classrooms—develop their own procedures for self-assessment and/or for assessing children's progress. Usually this is a staff activity, and does not include parents.

In addition to whatever self-evaluations centers develop, the State Department of Education *requires* self-assessment in compliance with forms that it has developed. However, two of Oakland's 24 Children's Centers have refused to comply with this state request, objecting that many of the questions asked are invasions of privacy. "We don't think it's necessary," says Bertha Canton of Centro Infantil, "to have all this information to plan an educational program—on home environment, mental health, pre-natal care, whether or not the child has books at home, whether or not the child relates more to adults or to children at home."

Moreover, some groups contend that the State assessment assumes the primacy of certain values which are antithetical to those of minority cultures—for example, placing an emphasis on individual achievement instead of sharing and cooperative behavior.

The total Children's Centers program is profiled annually in a descriptive report prepared by the Research Department of the Oakland Unified School District. This evaluation is based in large part on questionnaires sent to parents and teachers within the centers, and represents a major planning document for the program.

****

Extended Day Programs, Brookline, Massachusetts

SYNOPSIS

After-school care in Brookline, Massachusetts, represents an important model of parent control within the public school system.

Now operating in all eight of Brookline's elementary schools and in a facility attached to the Brookline Early Education Project (BEEP), the Extended Day Program—as it is called—serves some 358 children without regard to family income.

Each program is designed and administered by a separate parent group as a private not-for-profit corporation, yet all programs operate as part of the Brookline Public Schools in accordance with guidelines adopted by the School Committee. In effect, after-school day care in Brookline is a quasi-public school institution supported and regulated to some extent by the Board of Education but with considerable autonomy and variety among individual programs.

Paralleling Brookline's Extended Day Program is an Activities Program which offers students some 15-20 cultural and craft activities after school. Although they operate nominally under the auspices of the Extended Day parent corporations in each school, the Activities Program is really run by a separate set of parents. Activities are offered in 1½ hour blocks, and designed as an enrichment to the school curriculum. Because the Activities Program is not really a day care program, it is not included in this profile.

SERVICE DATA

Extent of Service

Number:	9 programs (8 in elementary schools, 1 at BEEP)
Hours of Operation:	11:15 AM-2 PM (3 programs)
	11:15 AM-5:30 or 6 PM (6 programs)
	No summer programs; during other school vacations and holidays, one of the nine remains open for use by all.

Children

Number Using Program:	358
Eligibility:	Attendance at local school.
	First-come, first-serve, in seven of nine programs; one program gives preference to children of working parents, another to children who attend all five days of the week.

Financing and Costs

Parent Fees:	6 programs flat-rate with scholarships (average full-time fee $28 per week).
	3 programs sliding-fee scale, $20-$33 per week.
Department of Public Welfare:	30 children
School Department:	Space, utilities, custodial services
	Custodial services costed at $18,930 out of total school budget of $14,601,091.

Personnel

Certification:	None required; staff are employees of private nonprofit corporations.
Salaries:	Directors ($5.75-$6.00 per hour); Teachers ($3.50-$5.50 per hour); paid per hours worked; benefits in only one of nine programs.

HISTORY AND DEVELOPMENT

Unlike all other programs profiled in this report, Brookline's Extended Day Program owes most of its development—and its continuation—to parents. For it is parents in need of child care who started the town's first two school-based after-school care programs in September 1972; and in September 1976, when the town had nine different programs, including one in each elementary school, it was parents who retained major control.

Moreover, the role of the Brookline Public Schools as the program's administrative sponsor has emerged, over the years, in response to the needs of its individual parent-run programs; i.e., in Brookline, unlike some other localities, there never was any intent or plan for public school involvement in day care.

What, then, brought extended-day care to be an official part of the Brookline schools?

Initial impetus came in January 1972, when a school principal, Mrs. Virginia Thompson, now retired, called a meeting of single parents with children in the Driscoll Elementary School to find out if they had a need for some form of child care; she was concerned about all the children she saw "hanging around" outside at the end of the day.

"I don't think any of us would have thought of using the public schools for child care if she hadn't suggested it as a possibility," says Pat Lynch, a parent who became one of the key developers of the program. "She said she'd go to the School Committee and get approval if we were willing to do the work."

Like Pat Lynch, many of the parents who showed up at the meeting were dissatisfied with the after-school arrangements they had for their children. Babysitters were erratic; "It's hard," one parent said, "to get a teenager to come every day." Center-based care was rare, uneven in quality, and expensive; Lynch was paying $35 per week for a program that she needed, but that made her feel very uncomfortable.

A questionnaire sent shortly after the meeting to all parents at Driscoll School found thirty single-parent *and* two-parent families with an immediate child care need, and a small committee of parents began doing the *work* that Mrs. Thompson spoke of. Within three months their planning prompted two parents at another Brookline school—Devotion—to seek their principal's commitment to the development of a child care needs survey, which found ten families interested in a program.

From the Devotion School's first meeting and child care questionnaire until the establishment, four years later, of after-school child care in all eight Brookline elementary schools, the pattern of program development has remained the same. A small group of parents who need child care have, with the approval of the principal, done a needs survey. While they set about incorporating and recruiting prospective consumers, the principal has sought out school space, often by enlisting the willingness of a kindergarten teacher to share a room. In several cases, parents from one school have sought advice from the Brookline Child Care Coordinator and from parents from programs that are already operating. For example, when a parent at Lincoln School wanted to start after-school care ("I needed it and I knew the area needed it"), she invited parents from the Driscoll and Devotion programs to talk to parents at Lincoln. In each case the need for and feasibility of child care at the particular school has been presented for approval by the School Committee, which, in its desire to maximize community use of tax-supported school facilities, has been generally enthusiastic about the programs. (Establishing programs has not always been without difficulty; in one particular case the principal wanted nothing to do with it but finally conceded that the parents could run their own program in his school.)

The first two after-school programs (Driscoll and Devotion schools) began operating in September 1972, with School Committee approval. However, they were not considered part of the Brookline school system; they had no formalized administrative relationship to the schools or any financial support beyond the provision of space and custodial services during those hours when custodians would normally be servicing the rest of the building (for additional hours, the programs paid the custodial cost, at time-and-a-half). The shift to public school sponsorship occurred as a response to regulatory technicalities that threatened to close the day care programs down.

Brookline's after-school care programs presented a quandary to several licensing authorities. In the absence of state regulations specifically covering day care programs for school-aged children, those for preschool children—with expensively high staff/child ratios—seemed to apply. The Fire Department code seemed to indicate that buildings were safe for children while they were in "school" (until 2 PM), but not safe after 2 PM when they were in "day care." According to the zoning code, the front half of Driscoll School was in a commercial zone; the back half, where the after-school classroom was located, was in a residential zone, and it was illegal to operate a business such as day care in a residential zone.

In a meeting of all the pertinent town departments, two School Committee members who were ardent supporters of the after-school programs offered the only practicable solution (without changing zoning ordinances, state regulations, etc.): make the day care programs—if in name only—part of the public schools. Once they became the "Extended Day Program of the Brookline Public Schools," day care regulations didn't apply.

(Deleting the "day care" title satisfied more than the regulatory agencies. Stigma about day care was such that School Committee members who wanted to gain popular support for the program didn't want it to be called "day care." As one parent says, "It's like a collective fiction maintained by everybody but the parents who use the program; they know it's day care." The public schools in Arlington, Virginia, operate an Extended Day program—not "day care"—for much the same reasons.)

Increased financial commitment, like official public school adoption of the programs, also developed as a response to a problem that threatened the programs in their beginning stages. According to the initial agreement, the schools would contribute space, utilities, and custodial services while *regular* school programs were in session: which meant that one of the programs soon found itself in financial crisis, obliged to pay $50-$60 overtime per week for custodial services provided between 5 and 6 PM. As a rescue measure, the public schools assumed the full custodial cost.

If the schools were going to adopt the programs and increase their financial support, it became clear that a more formalized agreement was needed, especially in view of the burgeoning interest at other schools where parents wanted to develop after-school programs. Under the aegis of a 4-C committee, a group including two school committee members, as well as parents and teachers from after-school programs developed a set of "Guidelines for Operation of Extended Day Programs in the Elementary Schools as Part of the Public School Program," which the full School Committee adopted. By the fall of 1976, with two more years' operating experience and with some form of extended-day program in all of Brookline's elementary schools, the guidelines were revised and expanded, providing a detailed framework for the operation of independent programs within the public school system *and* a commitment by the schools to include "specific space designated for Extended Day basic space" in all future building plans.

The Extended Day Program in Brookline has already attracted national attention: 1976 articles in *McCall's* and *Ladies Home Journal* prompted over 1,000 inquiries from towns across the country that want to develop after-school programs. Brookline's Superintendent of Schools, Dr. Robert Sperber, believes that one reason for the town's *increasing* school population is the provision of after-school child care; indeed, after-school care directors mention calls from new families in town who mistakenly think that they are automatically eligible for *free* day care.

What will be the future of extended day in Brookline?

Aside from space, the commitment of additional school resources seems unlikely; so does any attempt by the schools to take a larger administrative role. However, the latest addition to the after-school program, the extended day program of BEEP, raises an interesting question. BEEP is a foundation-funded long-term experiment in early intervention-parent education. It began offering an extended-day component because of the increasing number of parents who can only participate in it if they have some fuller form of day care for their children. Results and recommendations from BEEP—which might affect educational planning in Brookline—are due in 1985; by then, any large-scale expansion of a BEEP-type program might be dependent on the provision of extended-day care.

ADMINISTRATIVE STRUCTURE

Each of the after-school programs in Brookline has been developed and is administered by a separate parent-controlled board, incorporated as a nonprofit organization. Each program hires its own staff, who are *not* public school employees.

However, a carefully detailed set of School Committee approved "Guidelines for the Operation of the Extended Day Programs in the Elementary Schools as Part of the Public School Program" prescribes the relationship between the individual programs and the overall school administration (delineated in the accompanying chart) and affects several aspects of program operation. The administrative structure maximizes parent control within a framework of checks and balances that protects the individual schools and the overall school system.

Distinctive characteristics of the Extended Day Program are:
1. Parent Boards retention of autonomy and responsibility for curriculum, tuition, eligibility determinations, staff hiring.
2. Close coordination with the school principal.

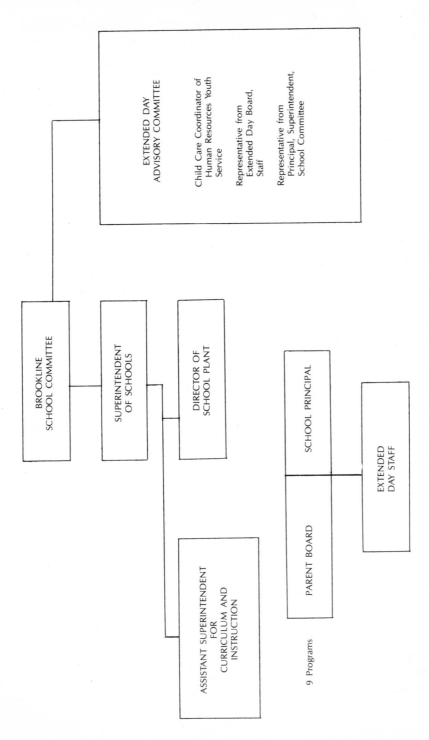

ADMINISTRATIVE STRUCTURE, BROOKLINE

3. School Committee involvement in program development.
4. Loose coordination among individual programs.

Parent Boards

Parent Boards—responsible for initiating, developing, and administering the after-school programs—are the backbone of the Extended Day Program in the Brookline Public Schools. They establish tuition rates and hire staff. As one parent said, "The program will not run without us."

Since each program is incorporated separately, requirements for board composition vary, as do the actual amounts of parental input and the relationships between the Board of Directors and the staff of the program. But only two programs have relatively low parental input. In one, the director, who has been with the program for four years while new parent board members have come and gone, is largely in charge and has to call meetings of the board. At the other extreme, one program operates almost like a co-op, requiring that every board member serve on an actively functioning committee that affects the daily life of the program; e.g., food purchasing, supplies, etc. In the remaining programs, parent boards delegate more responsibilities to their staff but still retain a very active hand in program operation. As one parent says, "We organized this child care program so we'd have time to work. Now we spend so much time running it that we still don't have time to work!"

Because parent commitment is so demanding, significant turnover in board membership occurs every year. Board members tend to burn out. In some programs, this creates transitional difficulties, but staff members and school principals observe that the turnover gives the programs "fresh blood" every year.

Coordination with School Principal

Extended Day Guidelines do not detail a supervisory role for the principal, but they do establish a framework for coordination: s/he *must* be a voting member of the Parent Board and *shall* interview prospective staff and make recommendations prior to hiring.

Although not stated as such, most programs construe the principal as having veto power over staff appointments. Since the operation of the programs depends to such a great extent on access to school facilities and the support of other school staff, it would not be politic for Parent Boards to hire staff against the principals' recommendations.

Disagreement between principals and Parent Boards rarely occurs. In one instance where it did, the Board deferred to the principal's wishes. According to the president of the Parent Board, "There really wasn't that much difference between the two top candidates. We would have been happy with either one."

Actual involvement of principals on the Parent Boards varies from school to school. In some, the principal judges (usually approvingly) on the recommendations of the rest of the Board. In others, the principal attends all meetings, and participates in all decision-making. Several principals feel strongly about guaranteeing program quality by making sure that the right personnel are hired. One makes a distinction between "professionals" and people with a "day care mentality" who think you just leave everything up to the classroom. Another says, "My primary concern is that this program is run well. There are a lot of schlock day care centers around. I want a classy operation. The best way to ensure that is to pick the appropriate personnel. The biggest impact I have on the day care program is making sure the people coming into it know what they're doing. I don't want to run a mere custodial operation. Sometimes that's all the parents want, but I want more than that. The fact that they're in the building, that there are high aspirations and expectations in the Brookline school system, carries over into day care." In all cases, the principal is ultimately responsible for everything that goes on within his or her building.

School Committee Involvement

According to the Guidelines, the Board of Directors of each program must include, ex-officio, a member of the School Committee.

While School Committee members do not, in fact, attend many individual Board Meetings, this structural provision reflects significant involvement of members of the Committee (the highest ranking group for educational policy making), rather than the School Department, in program development. (A current member of the School Committee was the parent organizer of the third after-school program to be established.) In effect the School Committee has been an enthusiastic advocate of the extended-day concept while the School Department—which has to live with daily operational issues—has been somewhat more conservative in its endorsement.

Loose Coordination of Programs

Each after-school program operates autonomously as a separate nonprofit corporation; there is no School Department ruling that the programs have to coordinate their efforts. However, School Committee Guidelines *allow for* the yearly establishment of an Extended Day Program Advisory Committee, consisting of a staff member and parent from each program, a school principal, the Superintendent of Schools (or his designee), a member of the School Committee, and the Child Care Coordinator of the Brookline Human Relations Youth Resource Commission. The Child Care Coordinator, who is an employee of neither the public schools nor the individual programs, convenes the committee on a monthly or bi-monthly basis to—

a. Aid parent groups in schools lacking Extended Day Programs in setting up such programs.
b. Aid existing groups in sharing resources, ideas and problems in order to attain and maintain the highest possible standards of Extended Day Programs and to promote the intellectual, social, physical growth and health of the children enrolled.
c. Recommend to the School Committee modifications of the regulations set forth when deemed appropriate or wise to do so.

The Child Care Coordinator mediates the needs of the various programs to the school administration, and vice versa (she was instrumental, for example, in developing the Guidelines according to which the programs operate). The non-mandatory coordinating structure which she supervises is considered invaluable by the individual programs, by the School Department, and by the School Committee: it allows the programs to develop individually, but also provides a formal mechanism for the development of policies that affect all programs.

With expansion of the Extended Day Program to include nine individual programs, the demands on the Child Care Coordinator specific to the Extended Day Program have increased. The School Department is considering hiring a person to coordinate all programs that take place in the public schools but outside the regular curriculum.

FINANCING AND COSTS

The Extended Day Program is financed from three sources:

Parent Fees

Parent fees established by the Board of Directors are the major source of income for all programs and cover the cost of salaries (80%-90% of total budget), equipment, supplies, and telephone. Six programs operate on a flat-rate fee basis, charging from $25 to $29 per week for five days of child care for a kindergarten child (roughly 11:15 AM until 5:30 PM); three programs have a sliding-fee scale ranging from $20 to $33 per week. Tuition is proportionately lower for those children—first through fourth grades—who are not done with school until 2 PM. All programs reduce tuition for siblings by one-third to one-half. Flat-rate programs all make scholarships available.

The Public School contribution of space and utilities considerably reduces the cost of child care to parents. Five-day tuition for a kindergarten child at the Brookline Children's Center, a private nonprofit program which is the only alternative to the Extended Day program, is $40 per week.

School Department

The School Department provides the programs with classroom space (separate when available, otherwise shared), utilities, the full cost of custodial coverage on days when school is in session, and partial cost of custodial coverage on selected days when school is not in session.

The costs of space and utilities have not been factored out, but the budgeted custodial cost for 1976-77 is $18,930 out of a total school budget of $14,601,191 and a physical plant budget of $1,857,000 (.13% of total school budget; 1% of physical plant budget).

The cash contribution for custodial services, although small, has increased with the development of the program, and reflects the increasing commitment of the public schools to a program which operates beyond regular school hours. When the first after-school program began operating in 1972, there was no public school dollar commitment beyond space and utilities. However, because of a public school-labor union contract, one of the first after-school programs found itself paying some $50-$60 overtime for custodial services provided between 5 and 6 PM. This financial burden—which threatened the existence of the program—precipitated public school commitment to covering full custodial costs whenever school is in session. (It also precipitated renegotiation of the custodian's contract, allowing for fuller use of the buildings on a ''straight-time'' basis.)

School Department financing of custodial costs has now been extended on a shared basis to allow the programs to operate during selected vacation days and holidays when school is not in session. The School Department pays half the custodial costs on non-legal holidays when school is not in session; during vacations (except summer and Christmas, when none of the programs operate) the custodial cost at one school is shared 50-50 by the School Department and all eight after-school programs.

Future financial commitment of the School Department to the after-school programs is reflected in School Committee Guidelines, which stipulate that ''future building plans shall include specific space designated for Extended Day basic space.''

Department of Public Welfare

Thirty children enrolled in four of the Extended Day Programs are funded by the Department of Public Welfare. Total cash subsidy in 1976-77 was $33,000—split unevenly among four programs.

ELIGIBILITY

Eligibility policies are determined separately by the Board of Directors of each after-school program. In seven of the nine programs, eligibility is granted on a first-come, first-serve basis, without regard to parent's working status or any other criteria. In one program, preference is given to working parents, and in another, preference is given to children who are enrolled all five days of the week.

All programs reserve the right not to maintain a child in a particular program if there is not a compatible match. As to children with special needs, one program has adopted the following policy: "The issue of accepting children with special needs was considered. It was probable that there would be parents who would wish to enroll children whose needs might place excessive demands on the time and skills of the teacher-director. Inasmuch as the program would be supported by parent funding, special staffing for such children might place inordinate financial pressures on this group. The committee agreed that children with special needs would be referred to the appropriate public agency."

To prevent exclusion of children because of financial means, each flat-rate fee program has established a scholarship committee. No policy exists mandating scholarships for all children who could not otherwise attend, but the School Committee has expressed its strong concern to the programs that scholarships be made available as needed.

OPERATIONAL ISSUES

Program Content

All programs offer children a range of activities including arts and crafts, music, cooking, and athletics. Staff or parents with special skills sometimes provide specialized activities.

Staff

Staff are employees of private nonprofit corporations, hired by the Board of Directors with, in some cases, significant input by the school principal, who is also a Board member.

Criteria for employment vary from program to program. In most programs, a teaching degree is less important than experience working with children and a feeling by the parents that they and their children would be comfortable with that person. In one program, however, the principal was insistent on a "first-rate professional staff, preferably with teacher-training," whom he distinguished from people with a "day care mentality, loose hanging, who don't pay much attention to the fatigue level of kids, who think that the environment will take care of it all."

Staff salaries, set by the Board, vary from program to program; Directors earn between $5.75 and $6.00 per hour; teachers between $3.65 and $5.50 per hour. Very few benefits are provided; only one program contributes to health insurance for its director, who also receives two weeks' paid vacation.

Directors of programs that operate from 11:15 AM until 6 PM are hired as teaching directors, to work while the children are there; but in order to keep up with their administrative responsibilities, most arrive at 9 AM or before, time for which they are not paid. To relieve some of his responsibilities, one director has hired a teacher for two hours a day, out of his own salary, so that he will be able to keep up with the work.

While there is little turnover in directors, other staff average about two years, in part because of their low salaries. The only alternatives to increasing staff salaries are to increase parent tuitions or for the public schools to take over the hiring and payment of after-school staff, a situation which is most unlikely at this point.

Coordination with Elementary School

There are several areas of interface between the after-school programs and the regular elementary school program: after-school staff are not employees of the public school, yet they must arrange for the use of school space (gym, home economics room, etc.), maintain a program of aceptable quality, and share space with public school teachers. Coordination between the elementary school and after-school program varies; in almost all instances described below the principal plays a key role.

• **Finding Space:** Nationally, elementary enrollment is decreasing, freeing up classrooms for other uses. In Brookline, however, elementary enrollment has increased over the last several years.

School principals have—first and foremost—to find space for the Extended Day Program. In one school, a girls' locker room has been partially converted for the after-school program, providing a small, but very warm and comfortable atmosphere; in another school, the principal put the music teacher on a rotating shift, allocating classroom space exclusively to the Extended Day program. Where separate space is not available—and it is not in three schools—the after-school programs must share space that is used earlier in the day by other classes, usually a kindergarten class; in one school, the cafeteria is the home base for the program, which utilizes the gymnasium and playground as well. While principals will not force their staff to share classrooms, they mediate its cooperative use; in one case, a principal made one of the criteria for hiring a new kindergarten teacher her willingness to share her room with another group.

The sharing of space has proved to be a difficult problem wherever it has been necessary. One program was required to move three times during the course of the year until a permanent base could be found in the elementary school building. In all cases, sharing requires a close working relationship between the morning teacher and the afternoon staff. The formation of such relationships takes time; as one after-school director explained, "When we started out last year, we weren't allowed to use the paints. After a few months, when she saw that we were acting responsibly, we got to use the paints. Now we share everything." In another case, where the after-school children were not allowed to use the many appealing toys in the kindergarten room, the teacher found that the energy devoted to prohibiting children from using the toys did not offset the advantage of a larger room, so he shifted to a smaller available room.

For the children in the elementary school classes, the sharing of space presents problems as well. Projects—such as elaborate block structures—cannot be continued from day to day when space is being used in the afternoon. And when children remain in the same classroom after school, it becomes essential—lest they become confused—to maintain the same general class rules.

A School Department report on the "Impact of the Extended Day Activities on the School Program" prepared in June 1976 found that the most serious "area of concern" regarding the operation of after-school programs in the schools was the use of shared space, in part because it necessitated that teachers put away regular classroom materials at the end of the day and then set up again each day.

Revised School Committee Guidelines adopted in the fall of 1976 recognize the space problem: "If at all possible, space used for regular classrooms during the day should not be assigned as basic (homeroom) space for Extended Day Programs. To this end, future building plans shall include specific space designated for Extended Day basic space." As this report was going to press, the Brookline School Committee voted a $20,000 appropriation for the 1979 fiscal year for renovations that would allow the extended-day program in one school to have its own separate space.

• **Elementary School Staff:** According to the director of one after-school program, "doing public relations with the school staff is three-quarters of my job." Or as one principal put it, "it took me a whole year to get them to accept an alien group." In most schools, day care is—or was—an alien presence: non-certified personnel are sharing classroom space and other school facilities for a purpose that many elementary school teachers find questionable. Some teachers complained, for example, that children in day care are too tired during the regular school day.

In the area of teacher relations, as with the sharing of space, the principal and the day care director play key roles in facilitating coordination. Where principals are supportive of day care, initial teacher resistance to day care has largely subsided. One day care director has facilitated school-wide cooperation by offering the Extended Day's film program to the whole school, holding a special screening once a month.

• **Evaluation of Children:** In most instances, no formal procedures exist for the comparison of child behaviors within the elementary school classroom and the day care setting, but such information-sharing takes place on an informal as-needed basis. Guidance counselors are instrumental in fostering such sharing, often asking both the school teacher and the day care teacher to discuss a particular child.

In one program, parents sign a written release if they want to permit the after-school staff to discuss their child with the elementary teacher and have access to school records.

• **Access to Other School Services or Facilities:** Access to all school facilities—e.g., home economics cooking area, gymnasium—is arranged via the principal. In most schools there is a regular schedule for use of these spaces by the after school program.

When available to the whole school population, the school nurse and doctor are also available to the after-school children.

Parent Involvement

The high degree of parent involvement in most of the after-school programs leads, according to principals at those schools, to increased parent involvement with the rest of the elementary school program: "I think it carries over to some degree into the regular classroom. If you're making decisions about day care, the expectation carries over that you can make decisions about the first grade."

From the school administrator's point of view, parent involvement also carries over to the regular classroom. As one principal says, "The parents have much more understanding of how the school works, of what goes into running a quality program, that they wouldn't have had otherwise."

Parents who have been involved with Extended Day recognize—and even complain—about the demands of running their programs. But as one parent said, "I feel I have more access to the school. It's much more a part of my life. I feel free now to call the principal's office if I have to, whereas before I didn't."

Program Evaluation

Although the after-school programs operate as part of the public schools, staff are not public school employees, and there is no formal mechanism for program evaluation. The principal of each school is implicitly responsible for the quality of all programs in his or her school and, as a mandatory member of the Parent Board, can bring to Board attention any concerns about the program. Most programs operate on the premise that if something is wrong, the principal will call attention to it.

In some programs, however, the Board has initiated a self-evaluation process; questionnaires to parents, Board members, staff, and the principal attempt to assess the program's success in meeting the needs of children and families, as well as the ability of individual staff. In one program, staff hold regular conferences with individual children to get feedback on the program. And in another, the principal will, in addition to the Board evaluation, prepare a written report on the program.

THE PROGRAM MODEL AND PUBLIC SCHOOL CONTROL

The Brookline Extended Day Program represents an interesting model of day care delivery in the public schools. Contribution of public school space and the modest cost of custodial services increases use of tax-supported school facilities and reduces the child care costs to parents. The administrative structure of the program maximizes parent responsibility and control while providing a framework that protects the individual school and the overall school system.

An increase in the public school administrative role and financial participation has occurred, over a four-year period, in response to particular program crises. However, no one I spoke to felt it would be desirable to increase School Department control of the program. Extended Day staff felt that the advantages to them of becoming school employees—higher salaries and benefits—would be outweighed by the effects on the program: loss of autonomy. School Department administrators felt that any more formalized school responsibility for monitoring program quality would not be feasible and would compromise parent involvement. While Parent Board members felt that an increased role for the schools might help provide stability and some welcome relief for the large amount of time they devote to the program, none wanted to give up *their* program. (Many felt, however, that it would be desirable to formalize the coordination among programs which is currently carried out on an *ad hoc* basis by the Child Care Coordinator for the Town of Brookline, who is not paid out of the public school budget. All felt it desirable, wherever possible, for the schools to provide separate space for the Extended Day Programs.)

Following is a sampling of comments from parents, school administrators, and Extended Day staff regarding increased school control of the Extended Day Program:

Cost to Schools

"The community has made a tremendous dollar investment in these facilities; we should make them available whenever we can."

(Superintendent of Schools)

Program Quality

"Short of taking over the whole program, this is the only way we could go." (Assistant Superintendent for Curriculum and Instruction)

Making Extended Day Directors School Employees

If the School Department hired the director, the tendency of the parents would be to let the director do everything, just like they do with the classroom teachers."

(Parent)

"If the schools took it over, you'd get paid for a full day of work; then again, the program would get caught up in all the school's red tape. It would take me months to order supplies I can get by going out to the store."

(Program Director)

"I wouldn't want the School Department hiring our personnel. The needs of an after school program are very different from those of a regular school program."

(Parent, Board President)

"I think you lose something if the school system takes this over, first in terms of the kind of people you get if you institutionalize hiring of people to run these kinds of programs. You might get the wrong kind of person."

(Superintendent)

"It wouldn't work to just extend School Department benefits. If you used a technicality to make them eligible for benefits, if you made them technical employees, the technicality of employment would soon become the reality of employment."

(School Committee Member)

Parent Involvement

"I think the schools are expected to do too much already, to solve every social problem. In terms of getting parent involvement, this is a very good model to have."

(Principal)

"This builds up a constituency of parents who feel they have a direct vested interest in the public schools. Parents are very concerned about the quality of adult contact of this day care for their children. Were the schools to run it, you wouldn't have that vested interest."

(Superintendent of Schools)

****

Comprehensive Child Day Care Program, Atlanta, Georgia

SYNOPSIS

The Comprehensive Child Day Care Program in Atlanta is one of the most extensive day care programs operated by a public school system in any city in the United States. Contribution of public school space and other certified public expenditures makes it possible to provide day care for some 3,535 Title XX children—64 percent of all such children currently enrolled in day care in Atlanta.

Operating in 34 elementary schools and one high school, the three-phased program includes: Prekindergarten care for infants (at one site) through five-year-olds; Expanded Day care for kindergarten students; and Extended Day care for school-aged children. All programs are administered as an integral part of the Atlanta Public Schools system, and all employees are school personnel.

Although the basic objective of Title XX day care, determined by federal guidelines, is to enable parents to seek or maintain employment or training, there is a strong emphasis in Atlanta on using day care as a means of early intervention and on achieving and measuring educational objectives. According to Dr. Juanita Whatley, Senior Operations Analyst for the Division of Research and Evaluation, "We cannot operate a program just for social service. The Board of Education wouldn't allow that and we are not a social service agency."

Credentialing and salary policies reflect the professional education model: 29 of 33 teachers have Master's or equivalent degrees and earn almost twice as much as teachers in Atlanta's private nonprofit centers.

As this report went to press, financial constraints were leading Atlanta towards significant changes in its staffing patterns. As of July 1, 1978, some 50% of the teacher positions (head teacher in most other programs) will be eliminated. And in the next fiscal year, beginning July 1, 1979, all teacher positions will be phased out; centers will then be headed by paraprofessionals who now meet the requirements for "group leader": two years of post-high school training in early childhood education at either community college or vocational school.

SERVICE DATA (1976-1977)

Extent of Service

Type and Number of Programs:	35 Prekindergarten for children aged 3 to 5, including one program serving infants and toddlers, one high school laboratory program, one outreach program.
	29 Expanded Day for kindergarten children before and after their half day of public school.
	29 Extended Day for school-aged children before and after their regular school day.*
Hours of Operation:	7:00 AM to 6:00 PM
	Prekindergarten day care operates all year, including school vacations and summer; other programs operate only during school year.
Eligibility:	Title XX.

Children

Number Using Program:	3,535 total in 1976-77.
	1580 Prekindergarten
	810 Expanded Day
	1145 Extended Day
Percentage of Title XX Day Care Children in Atlanta:	64 percent (3,535 out of 5,566)

Financing and Costs

Total Budget:	$5,063,497
Board of Education:	Certified In-kind (space, utilities, etc): $1,265,874 per year (pro-rated from nine month certified expenditure of $949,466)

---

*The Extended Day program was eliminated in Fall 1977, a step taken by the Atlanta Public Schools to cut its budget without cutting overall services too drastically. Of the three program components, Extended Day was the least in demand, especially during the summer.

Georgia Department of   Title XX (Federal): $3,797,623 per year
  Human Resources: (pro-rated from nine-months budget of
                             $2,936,339)

Parent Fees: Free for family of four up to $7,800 annual
                             gross; sliding-fee scale as of January 1,
                             1977, extends eligibility to $10,932 annual
                             gross. For a family of four, fees will range
                             from $1 per week at gross income of $697
                             per month to $20 per week at $911 per
                             month.

Cost Per Child
Prekindergarten: $2,368 (12 months)
Expanded Day: $ 919 (9 months)
Extended Day: $ 333 (9 months)

Personnel
Certification: All staff are employees of the Atlanta Public
                             Schools. Minimum requirement for
                             teachers: B.A. in early childhood or
                             elementary education plus three years of
                             teaching experience.
Salaries: Separate scales for professionals (teachers)
                             and paraprofessionals (group leaders and
                             aides). Teacher scale with B.A. ranges
                             from $10,932 per year to $17,088 per year
                             in 16 steps; with M.A. from $12,024 to
                             $18,792. Salaries are for 12 months work
                             in full-day care.
                          Paraprofessional salary range:
                             Group Leaders - $6564 per year to $8040 per
                             year in seven steps
                             Aides Rank I - $5472 per year to $6696 per
                             year in seven steps
                             Aides Rank II - $6012 per year to $7368 per
                             year in seven steps

HISTORY AND DEVELOPMENT

Since its inception in 1969, the day care program in the Atlanta Public
Schools has been predicated on the rationale that early learning is critical
for the prevention of later deficits. The role of the schools, then, is not
just to care for children, but to educate them with highly trained staff.

According to Dr. Jarvis Barnes, Assistant Superintendent for Research and Evaluation, "The Federal people view this as a program for parents to work and be trained; we have viewed it as that plus an opportunity for the education of children." Coupled with that "opportunity"— and distinctively characteristic of the Atlanta Public Schools day care program—is an ongoing attempt to *measure* children's gains as a way of justifying Board of Education expenditures on day care.

As one of three cities in Georgia with a locally supported kindergarten (since 1922), Atlanta has long been interested in the education of young children. But large-scale involvement of children below five years of age did not begin—as in many other communities throughout the country— until Head Start funds became available in 1965. At that time, the Atlanta Public Schools established a Research and Evaluation unit, as one administrator says, "to see what could best be done with funds."

"We made the decision then," says Dr. Barnes, "to focus on prevention rather than remediation. We began to focus on the early grades— first, second, and third—with Title I in September 1965. After a year of operating and analyzing the data, we found that we had to start earlier. In September 1966, we used Teacher Corps money to focus on kindergarten. During this period, we realized we had to focus earlier than kindergarten, so we set up four Title I preschool centers for four-year-olds. We also had Parent-Child centers under the Economic Opportunity Act. The whole process began to show us that parents had to be involved in the process and we had to do it on a broader basis."

When Federal monies for day care first came to Atlanta via Model Cities in 1969, the public schools became one of two subcontractors, operating programs for four year olds in nine elementary schools. In terms of educational philosophy, public school day care in Atlanta was a logical extension of the Title I preschool programs: readying children for the school experience. In terms of fiscal reality, as one school board member put it, "We got into it because the money was there." From the outset, the educational aspects of public school day care were stressed, even in subtle ways: while non-public school programs received "technical assistance" from the local 4-C's (Community Coordinated Child Care), public school programs received "staff training" from Atlanta University.

Open-ended Title IV-A funding in February 1971 brought the possibility of vast expansion of public school day care in Atlanta. It also brought opposition: private nonprofit providers were afraid that the public schools would put them out of business. In concern for control of the day care "turf," the Atlanta 4-C's played a mediating role: a 4-C's survey indicated that there was more need than could be supplied by the public schools. But it was also true that the public schools were more readily able than any other agency to provide the IV-A matching funds through "certified public expenditures." By the end of 1972, day care was being provided in 39 of Atlanta's schools.

The December 1972 Congressional ceiling on Title IV-A expenditures "pulled the rug out from under us," according to Dr. Barnes. "We had submitted $16 million worth of proposals for every type of day care program, even nightime nurseries. Then they put the lid on, told us to work only with the welfare eligible, and gave us 1,001 different regulations to follow." Ms. Jacquelyn Cook, then head of the Atlanta 4-C's, observes that "the lid on IV-A funding probably prevented a monolithic situation from occurring."

Still the public schools are a major provider of day care in Atlanta: they operate 35 of the 70 Title XX contracted programs in the Metropolitan Atlanta area, and serve 64 percent of all Title XX children in day care. For their efforts in FY '77, the schools received $3,797,623 in Title XX funds through the Georgia Department of Human Resources; total DHR funding for all other metropolitan-wide day care programs combined was $3,577,009.*

The future of public school day care in Atlanta is directly tied to Federal funding. As in many communities, fiscal pressures are taking their tolls on the schools; 11 were closed in the last two years because of utility expenses. A fixed appropriation of $3,797,623 Title XX funds from the Georgia Department of Human Resources, combined with annually escalating salaries and school operating costs, means that something has to go. In the past, it has been the children: the number served has decreased from 3,840 in 1972 to 3,535 in 1976. (Staff has also been reduced in proportion to children.)

Now, the Atlanta Public Schools are wondering if there are not other approaches to balancing costs and services. The underlying rationale for Atlanta's day care program is "educational"; indeed, all school tests show that children in day care come to school better prepared than their non-day care counterparts. But gains do not seem to be sustained by the end of kindergarten, raising fundamental questions about the allocation of public education resources for day care.[†]

How can the "measurable gains" of day care be sustained? Attempts are being made to better coordinate the Expanded Day and Kindergarten programs, so that concepts learned in Kindergarten are reinforced in Ex-

---

*Both figures are for 12 months of operation; the public school figure is pro-rated from a nine-month budget of $2,936,339.

[†]According to Dr. Juanita Whatley, Research Associate for the Atlanta Schools, "First and second grade test data (*Iowa Tests of Basic Skills*) indicate that day care children perform as well as or slightly better than students who have not had day care. Data indicates that comparable low-income group of students who had not been in day care did not perform as well as day care students so the gains have not been completely lost. Continued longitudinal study for the third grade in 1977 will be especially significant since this is the level where the regular student population test results begin to decline."

panded Day. But administrators are also questioning the necessity—if gains on tests wash out—of employing such highly credentialed and expensive teachers in day care. Perhaps such an emphasis on education credentials is unnecessary. Perhaps new measures of children's progress are needed, so that day care is not called into question when "cognitive gains" appear to evaporate. Or perhaps the data are suggesting that children "learn more" with adult support, that the shift from Federally mandated staff/child ratios of one to seven in day care to kindergarten classes with one teacher and 28 five-year-olds prevents the continuation of cognitive gain.

Given the educational rationale underpinning its extensive day care program, the way that Atlanta resolves these issues may prove critical for it, and for other public school systems, in the next few years.

ADMINISTRATIVE STRUCTURE

The Comprehensive Child Day Care Program is administered as an integral part of the Atlanta Public Schools system, within the existing administrative structure. All personnel are public school employees, and most program functions—e.g., purchasing, hiring, evaluation, curriculum determination—are centralized. Four area-wide Advisory Committees, composed 50 percent of parents with children enrolled in the program, provide a structure for parent involvement; however, their function is strictly advisory.

Distinctive characteristics of Atlanta's administrative structure can be found in—

1. System-wide Administration: Area-wide Supervision and Centralized Coordination
2. On-site Administration: Principals and Teachers.
3. Parent Advisory Councils
4. Function of Research and Evaluation

System-wide Administration: Area-wide Supervision and Centralized Coordination

As the accompanying organizational charts indicate, Atlanta's public schools are divided into four areas, each with its own Superintendent.

---

* As this report went to press, Atlanta decided that it could not afford the cost of its highly credentialed teachers. Beginning on July 1, 1979, all centers will be headed by paraprofessionals who now meet the requirements for "group leader": two years of post high school training in early childhood education at either community college or vocational school.

Responsibility for the day care program is delegated along two major administrative lines: as a "special service" with its own system-wide Project Director, and as an area-wide program, under the supervision of each Area Superintendent.

The Project Director has major responsibility for the *planning, coordination,* and *evaluation* of the operation of the day care program throughout the system; however, the Project Director has no line authority for supervision of staff. The Area Superintendents have responsibility for the *implementation* of all day care programs within their area.

Coordination between the central Project Director and the Area Superintendents is facilitated by Area Resource Teachers, who work from the office of—and are directly responsible to—their Area Superintendents. Resource Teachers are the coordinating "field staff" for all day care programs within each area; they work with teachers as "resources" for staff training and curriculum development; they work with principals as informal program evaluators; and they work with parents, organizing area-wide parent advisory councils. Although Resource Teachers are not directly responsible to the Project Director, they are, in effect, her field staff too; they meet with her regularly to provide input for overall program planning.

On-site Administration: Principals and Teachers

Responsibility at the individual school level is shared by the day care "teacher"—who teaches three hours per day and administrates for five—and the school principal, who has ultimate responsibility for all programs within the building. There is no separate day care director for each program, although from 1971-75, each program had a "lead teacher" whose duties were primarily administrative.*

The flavor or tone of each program is very much set by the style of the teacher and the involvement of the principal, which varies significantly from school to school. As one teacher put it, "Just as a school reflects the principal's philosophy, so the day care located in the school reflects that philosophy."

One example—admittedly unique—illustrates the role the principal *can* play. When Title IV-A funds for day care first became available, Atlanta's elementary principals had the choice of offering or not offering

---

*In 1974, when the schools underwent a major reorganization, lead teacher positions were abolished in day care and other school programs; in part this was for administrative clarification, and in part because the lead teacher arrangement was too expensive.

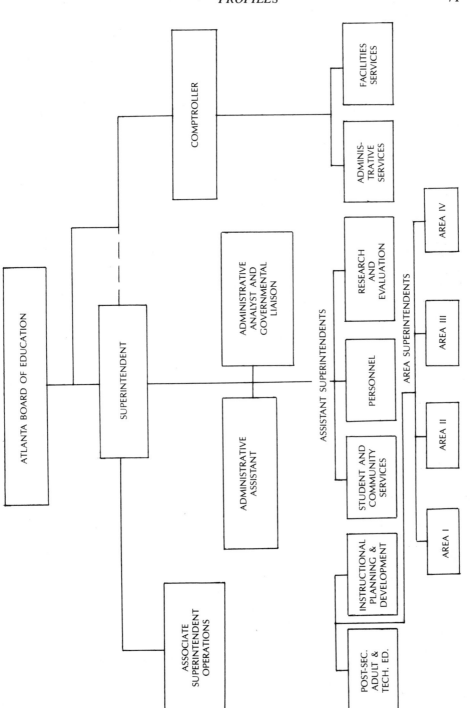

ORGANIZATION—ATLANTA PUBLIC SCHOOLS

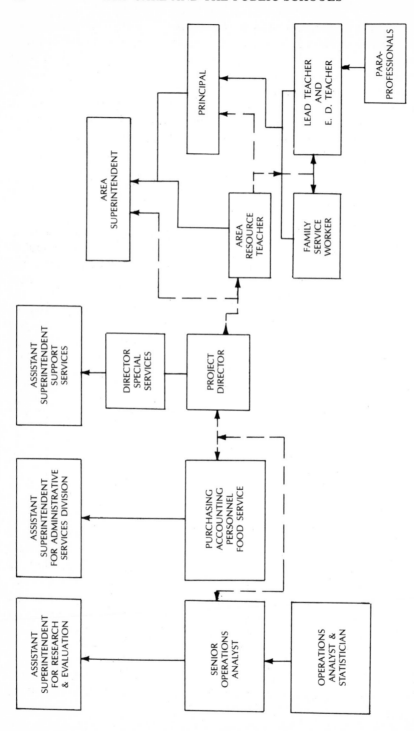

AREA LEVEL ORGANIZATION OF COMPREHENSIVE CHILD DEVELOPMENT PROGRAM, ATLANTA

their schools as program sites. In one school, however, the principal already had two years' experience in negotiating a school-related day care program. Because so many children enrolled in her school were at home taking care of younger siblings, the absentee rate was very high. So, the principal worked out an arrangement with the pastor of the neighborhood church—which ran a small day care program—that allowed children in her school to attend day care for only $5 per week, paid for by the parents. Within two years, inflation made it impossible for the church to charge anything less than $15 per week; but at that point, Title IV-A funding allowed the principal to continue her commitment to day care in her own school, where she takes a significant role in its administration: even before prospective day care parents see the family service worker for eligibility determination, they see the principal.

At its inception, day care was only located at schools where principals wanted it; however, the transfer rate of principals from one school to another or from one position to another is high. The role of principals varies considerably, depending in part on personal interest in, commitment to, or understanding of day care. In one school, for example, where the space for day care is physically separated from the principal's office by two flights of stairs, the center teacher sees the Area Resource Teacher more frequently than the principal. And in another, the teacher feels that the needs of young children have not been legitimized with the rest of the teaching staff: "We've been here four years and we still have teachers saying, 'Can't you keep those kids quiet?' and teachers who want us to enforce their method of discipline, who say, 'Why don't you just paddle the child?' "

Parent Advisory Committees

Advisory Committees established in each area and composed at least 50 percent of Title XX consumers provide a structure for parent input.

As the Atlanta Public Schools explain in their Title XX proposal, "The function of each committee is advisory, not governing. Their advice and views will be essential and will be given serious consideration when developing curriculum emphasis, planning activities, and reviewing operating procedures within the guidelines of federal and state regulations."

However, the extent to which the advice and views of parents are given consideration through the Advisory Committee structure varies considerably and depends, to a great extent, on parent leadership in each area. As the family service worker in one program says, "We just had an area wide meeting and five parents showed up. I think it's a problem inherent in the system, as opposed to individual centers. We don't have to depend on their input to keep going, so we don't try too hard to keep them involved." According to the teacher in another program, "The Advisory Committees can't change any policies. Most of the rules come from the Board of Education, and we follow; they don't have anything to say about the hiring or firing of staff."

Advisory Committees are scheduled to meet twice quarterly. The first four meetings are devoted to election of officers. "We're trying to get parents to come to all of the meetings," says one parent. "We were talking about the budget at the first one; I didn't really understand too much about it. At the second, we were electing officers for next year."

Some Advisory Committee meetings resemble parent meetings at the individual center level, designed for parent education rather than influencing the program. "Our last meeting was on how to keep burglars from breaking into your house," says one parent. "Before that a dentist talked about how to care for children's teeth. It's not specifically a mechanism for evaluating or bringing information about the programs."

Advisory Committees can have an impact, however. In one area, parents at one center worked for almost two years to prevent its anticipated closing. At the last minute they approached their Advisory Council, headed by a parent who is active in community affairs and now running for City Council. In a meeting with the Area Superintendent and Principal it was determined that the center would not be closed.

Research and Evaluation

From 1971 to 1974, there was no separate Project Director for the Comprehensive Child Day Care Program; instead, day care was operated from the Research and Evaluation unit of the Atlanta Public Schools, an administrative arrangement that highlights, perhaps, the program's continuing and distinctive emphasis on educational outcomes.

Although the Research and Evaluation unit no longer has any line authority over day care, it does have a significant relationship, one that bears on program administration. Charged with monitoring Title XX contract compliance, R&E research assistants visit programs every six weeks. Research and Evaluation staff are also responsible for writing and negotiating all Title XX proposals with appropriate state and federal officials and base their actions on recommendations from principals, resource teachers, and the Program Director.

FINANCING AND COSTS

The Comprehensive Child Day Care Program is funded by federal title monies matched by public school certified public expenditures.

	Cash Budget*	Certified Cost
1972-73	$3,220,750	$1,073,583
1973-74	3,250,300	1,083,433*
1974-75	3,646,650	1,215,550
1975-76	3,797,622	1,265,874
1976-77	2,936,339	978,780†

* 11 month budget
† 9 month budget

Beginning in January 1977, a sliding-fee scale added an additional source—though not an additional amount—of income: parents.

Federal Funding

Since its inception, financing of the Comprehensive Child Day Care Program has been dependent on federal funds. From 1972 to 1975, the Comprehensive Child Day Care Program was financed by Title IV-A, and since 1975 by Title XX. The level of federal funding has increased during that period from $3,220,750 in 1972 to $3,797,622 in 1975.

Federal funding is funneled to the Atlanta Public Schools via the Georgia Department of Human Resources according to the terms of a yearly purchase of service contract.

Atlanta Public Schools

The schools finance the day care program in two ways. They provide the required 25 percent matching share for Title XX as a certified public expenditure. And, they pay on a cash basis (1.5 percent or $58,727 for 1975-76) for Department of Human Resources overhead in administering Title XX funds.

Certified expenditures include the cost value of all services and facilities contributed to the Title XX program through the normal operation of the School System. They include the costs of space, depreciation of furnishings and equipment, and salary and non-salary (office supplies, materials) costs for all school personnel involved with the operation of day care—school superintendent, area superintendents, principals, school librarians, clerks, etc.

Additional public school expenditure for day care seems most unlikely in this time of fiscal constraint; even if the value of public school in-kind contribution were increased and if additional Title XX funds became available, the schools would have to use their own funds for renovations or other capital outlays. Eleven schools were closed in Atlanta in 1975 to reduce operating costs, particularly in neighborhoods where school populations had decreased significantly.

Parent Fees

A sliding-fee scale for consumers of Title XX day care was implemented in Atlanta on January 1, 1977. Fees for a family of four will begin at $1 per week where monthly gross income is $697 and extend to $20 per week where the monthly gross is $911.

Parent fees generated by the new system will not contribute to the financing of Title XX day care in any significant way by increasing the number of children who can be cared for or reducing Title XX expenditures.

Costs

Yearly per child costs for the three separate components of the Comprehensive Child Day Care Program break down as follows:

	Prekindergarten Day Care	Expanded Day	Extended Day
1975-76	$2,294*	$1,024	$461
1976-77	2,367*	919/9 mo	433/9 mo

* Projected to 12-months from 9-month proposal. Expanded and Extended Day should not be projected for 12 months since these are only 9-month programs.

Administrative costs represented 18 percent of the 1975-76 budget; instructional costs represented 82 percent.

ELIGIBILITY

Although the focus of the schools is on educating children, eligibility for day care is determined exclusively in compliance with Federal goals for Title XX day care service:

1. Achieving or maintaining *economic self-support* to prevent, reduce, or eliminate dependency.
2. Achieving or maintaining *self-sufficiency,* including reduction or prevention of dependency.
3. Preventing or remedying neglect, abuse, or exploitation of children and adults unable to *protect* their own interests, or preserving, rehabilitating, or reuniting families.

Family Service Workers assigned to each day care program determine eligibility according to the following guidelines:

1. Income Maintenance Status: recipient of AFDC or SSI.
2. Income Eligible Status: free service for family of four up to $7,800 gross per year.

3. Protective Service: without regard to income.

With implementation of the sliding-fee scale in Atlanta, income eligibility for a family of four will range from $697 to $911 per month.

There are no children in the program from other than Title XX eligible families; most non-public school Title XX day care programs in Atlanta are similarly income segregated. As the principal of one school says, "Every day we have calls from parents whose income is a little bit above the eligibility criteria. Without a sliding fee scale, as soon as people get above income, they have to drop right back down again."

PERSONNEL

All members of the teaching staff are employees of the Atlanta Public Schools. There are two major classifications of teaching staff: teachers, who have administrative responsibilities and who function, in effect, as teacher-directors; and group leaders and aides, who work exclusively with children. The two classifications are reflected in criteria and procedures for hiring, and salaries.

Criteria

The Atlanta Public Schools Comprehensive Child Day Care Program prides itself on the number of teachers with undergraduate and even graduate degrees. According to the Project Director, Ms. Emmalean Bonds, "The State doesn't require degreed people to head centers. We don't feel we could offer the same quality if we didn't have degreed people."

Minimum requirements set by the Georgia Department of Human Resources for directing or working in a day care center are "evidence of completing recent training (within three years) in the field of child care."

The minimum requirement for Atlanta Public Schools day care teachers who spend three hours in the classroom and five in administration is a bachelor's degree in early childhood education or a related discipline and four years' teaching experience. Of the 33 public school day care teachers currently employed, 23 have the M.A. and six have at least 35 credits beyond the M.A.

Teaching staff apart from the "teacher"—who is, in effect, a teaching director—are divided into two classifications: group leaders and aides. Group leaders have primary responsibility for children during the course of the day; minimum requirements for group leaders are two years of successful post-high school training at an accredited vocational technical school or a community college and a Rank II Aide license from the State Department of Education (more than the State requires). Most of Atlanta's group leaders come from Atlanta Area Tech; some have already earned the B.A. The minimum requirements for day care aides, who work under the supervision of the teacher, are a ninth grade education and a 90-hour course in child development. The level of credentialing required of Atlanta Public School aides is also more than the State of Georgia's minimum requirement for day care directors.

Procedures for Hiring

Hiring and assignment of all but part-time aides is done by a centralized personnel office, which assigns or reassigns personnel in accord with the needs of the total system.

When full-time positions are available, principals can make recommendations to their Area Superintendents, but for the most part neither school principals nor the day care teachers in charge of individual programs have much choice in staffing decisions.

According to one teacher, "They staff from a combined pool of paraprofessionals and aides and don't let you go out and hire the best people. If Title I aides are phased out they may be put into day care, whether or not they have day care experience or aptitude."

Several day care teachers, who have supervisory responsibility for the day-to-day operation of programs, state that the lack of flexibility in hiring is the major drawback of the public school system. "Our out-reach is a combination of education and social support," says one. "It requires a mature person to do it. Our paraprofessionals out of high school need support themselves. We need a bit more than high school graduates. We also need commitment. You've got to have commitment to do this, so you don't go out and drag your feet. We need somebody who cares enough to go back if the family wasn't at home. *We can't choose our own staff.*"

However, teachers also recognize that system-wide centralization of teaching assignments provides, through seniority and "bumping," the security that hampers flexibility: "I'm guaranteed a job based on my seniority; if Title XX were phased out and a kindergarten teacher had three years of experience and I had four, I would get that job. I'm certified K-7. I would get any elementary school job." *

Salaries

There are three separate pay scales for day care staff: one for teachers and two for personnel in the aide category (group leaders and aides).
Salary ranges in each category are:
1. Teachers:
   B.A. - $10,932 per year to $17,088 per year in 16 steps.
   M.A. - $12,024 per year to $18,792 per year in 16 steps.

---

*This statement is not entirely accurate; placement also depends on the availability of positions supported by general funds.

2. Group Leaders:
   $6,564 per year to $8,040 per year in seven steps.
3. Aides:
   Rank I - $5,472 per year to $6,696 per year in seven steps (minimum training)
   Rank II - $6,012 per year to $7,368 per year in seven steps (two years post-high school)

Salaries, especially those for day care teachers, are significantly higher in the public school program than in other day care programs in Atlanta. As one teacher says, "The average day care director in Georgia is making $8,000 to $9,000. I'm making almost double that."*

Salaries for day care staff, like other public school employees, increase automatically each year. By contrast, according to the representative from the Georgia Department of Human Resources who oversees the Title XX day care contract, staff at most other Title XX programs—private nonprofit and those operated by the city—have received no pay raises in three years.

Title XX funding carries with it no stipulation for staff salaries. In contracting with the Atlanta Public Schools, the Georgia Department of Human Resources accepted the school pay scale for day care, as it did the pay scale of a private agency, Sheltering Arms, in Atlanta. In contracting with the Atlanta Housing Authority, however, which had no salary scale for day care, DHR developed a salary scale in conjunction with the State merit system.

No data is available to indicate whether or not the higher salaries and guaranteed increments of the Atlanta Public Schools program lead to greater staff stability than in non-public school programs. However, because the Department of Human Resources does not increase its annual Title XX allotment, guaranteed salary increments strain other areas of the budget as well as the ability of the program to maintain the same level of service.

Concern for reductions in service is reflected in a study being conducted at the request of the School Department Cabinet—Superintendents and other top level administrators—to determine whether the same educational results can be achieved with less highly certificated personnel.[†]

---

*According to a Wage Comparability Study conducted in May 1976 by Economic Opportunity Atlanta, the salary range for Atlanta directors was $8,788 to $17,831.

[†]The study is being done by Abt Associates as a special phase of the National Day Care Center Study. However, as this report went to press, the School Department decided that fiscal constraints would not allow it to wait on study results; a decision was made to reduce the requirements for personnel.

CURRICULUM AND COORDINATION WITH ELEMENTARY SCHOOL

Providing children with an early learning experience that enhances their cognitive growth and readies them for school is a primary objective of Atlanta's Comprehensive Child Day Care Program. To sustain children's "gains" and provide continuity to their experience, the Atlanta Public Schools place a distinct emphasis on coordination of day care and elementary school programs. Several operational aspects of such coordination, all affected considerably by the principal, are these:

Grouping/Assignment of Children in Kindergarten

The way in which day care children are assigned to kindergarten classes is a seemingly small but significant aspect of program coordination. As one school principal says, "The transition to regular school is a beautiful thing. All the teachers want the kids who have been in day care. You don't have to get them ready for school because they've been a part of school." On the other hand, a few teachers find that children with day care experience are disruptive to their classes—they have already done the whole curriculum.

In response to these issues, several programs group all day care children in the same kindergarten room. In one school with two kindergarten teachers, the principal alternates the assignment of the day care class each year; in another, the principal assigns day care children to a class where the teacher has increased expectations of the children.

In still another, the principal takes an individualized approach with all children. Some four-year-old day care children in her school spend a portion of their day in kindergarten; some kindergarteners spend a portion of their day in first grade.

Curriculum Development

The "school-readiness" of day care children has become an issue not only for kindergarten assignment within individual schools, but for system-wide curriculum development. According to the Coordinator for Elementary Education, "We've had parent and teacher complaints that when the children get to kindergarten, they were doing the same things they had been doing for 1½ years. Day care has made a significant impact on our overall requirements and expectations of young children."

Some attempt is being made at centralized development of a coordinated curriculum, one that would account for the skills of day care children. However, according to the Coordinator, "it may be more of an intent than a reality. Day care staff (at the top level) are often involved in writing proposals; but it's difficult to coordinate because of the nature of the system."

Earlier attempts with a centralized curriculum do not bode well. The Board of Education invested in two costly curriculum packages—one for its Prekindergarten program, one for its outreach components—but neither is relied on to any significant extent by teachers. Prekindergarten teachers set "educational objectives" in conjunction with monthly themes; outreach teachers, having gone through two prepackaged curricula, now try to respond to the needs in each home.

Expanded Day and Elementary Curriculum

In an effort to sustain cognitive gains made by day care children, emphasis is being placed on coordinating the curriculum of all Expanded Day programs with that of the kindergarten. (Children spend about half their day in each of these programs.) Concepts presented in kindergarten are being systematically reinforced by teachers in the Expanded Day session, and time is set aside in each Expanded Day class for kindergarten "homework." Teachers in each program meet anywhere from one to three times a week, depending on the particular school and the extent to which the principal fosters the coordinated effort.

Record Keeping: Evaluation of Children

Methods of recording children's progress and transmitting records to kindergarten or elementary personnel vary considerably. Anecdotal observations are kept sporadically, at best, in some programs, more regularly in others. In some schools, the kindergarten teacher would never see a child's day care folder unless s/he requested it; it is kept at the day care program.* In others, a folder with anecdotal notes and all test results is forwarded automatically from day care and used by the kindergarten teacher, in consultation with the day care teacher, for kindergarten grouping of children.

The Coordinator of Early Childhood Education, responsible for grades K-3, has organized a committee of day care and elementary teachers to develop a "checklist that wouldn't say negative things about children and that would become the basis of a more systematic and regular process of coordinated evaluation."

---

*Dr. Juanita Whatley of the Atlanta Schools notes that, "It is a federal requirement that records be maintained at the Center for a minimum of five years. Developmental data are available for transfer. A more formalized system for transferring data from day care to kindergarten is being pursued for 1977-78.

PARENT INVOLVEMENT

Opportunity for parent involvement exists at two levels: via individual programs and via the Area Advisory Committees, already discussed under Administrative Structure.

At the center level, parents can be involved as classroom volunteers or paid aides, and they can attend monthly parent meetings.

Actual participation varies considerably from center to center, depending largely on the personality of the principal and/or teacher and the rapport established with the parents. According to one teacher, "Parents often come and help us. We invite parents all the time. When they come in we say we need hands; 80% of the parents work, but we catch them on holidays and days off. We have 67 families; for parent meetings we get 40 to 50 families. We hire college students to conduct groups—like exercise class, or education or using food commodities." According to another, "Parents are kind of indifferent; once in a while one will come to you and say thank you for what you've done. Those who come to raise sand do it because Johnny lost his mittens, not because you're not teaching him."

Several programs boast their major parent turnouts at a Christmas party and a spring picnic; indeed, center-level participation is most often for parties or other social events. "It's more of a getting together than any policy or advice," says one teacher.

Public school programs are not dependent on parent participation in the same way that some non-public school Title XX programs are. According to a staff member of the Department of Human Resources, who monitors both, "It's easier to get parents involved in the private non-profit programs. In the small centers, they know they have to be involved in money raising. The parents feel, if we don't do this, it will fail. In one center in particular, every two weeks they have something going on, like putting on fire-retardant paint."

But according to Ms. June Cofer, also in a position to observe both public and non-public school programs (she is a member of the Atlanta Board of Education and works for the Atlanta 4-C's organization), "Private centers aren't necessarily going to include parents in decision-making. It's six of one, half a dozen of the other; parents don't want to be involved that much anyway. We have Title XX centers where the director runs the whole show!"

MONITORING AND EVALUATION

Monitoring and evaluation of the Comprehensive Child Day Care Program can be divided into two broad areas which reflect the dual nature of the program: on the one hand, it is a Title XX social service program designed to allow parents to work while assuring a certain governmentally mandated standard of care; on the other, it is an educational program whose justification rests largely on proof of children's academic gains. Monitoring and evaluation are carried out by DHR and public school personnel; parents have no input in either process.

Contract Compliance

Responsibility for the monitoring of contract compliance and the maintenance of program quality is assumed by both the Georgia Department of Human Resources and the Atlanta Public Schools. DHR representatives "try to visit each center once per quarter," and provide monitoring reports to the center teacher, the principal, and the Area resource teacher. The monitoring function ranges from issues of record-keeping to classroom management—e.g., providing information about an aide who is having difficulties with a class. Research Assistants from the Atlanta Public Schools also visit the programs every six weeks, filing reports about compliance in areas such as staff/child ratio. Area Resource Teachers play a more informal monitoring function, passing along comments and technical assistance.

Child Development Goals

Perhaps the most distinctive feature of the Comprehensive Child Day Care Program is its emphasis—far beyond any Title XX or Georgia Department of Human Resources mandate—on child development goals. According to Dr. Juanita Whatley. "Our division is supposed to be able to say to the Board of Education, this program is worth having."

In addition, by pinpointing areas of gain or lack of gain, the Research and Evaluation Division is supposed to influence curriculum development for both day care and the elementary schools.

In its annual program report for 1976, the Research and Evaluation unit notes the difficulties of measuring children's developmental progress in any exact way: "The success and value of the day care program is difficult to quantify since a contract year is filled with many intrinsic successes and failures. Five-year-old Ellen learned to share her crayons, ten-year-old Mark walked away from a potential fight, Mrs. Brown got a better paying job, Mrs. Jones finally comes on time to pick up Billy, and 20 out of 30 families are represented at family night. These are the little successes that make up day care, but these are things that often go unrecorded."

Nevertheless, quantitative measurement is a major feature of the program. From the several tests administered during 1974-75—SREB Rating Scales, Basecheck, and Caldwell Preschool Inventory—it seems clear that children in day care make significant gains *but* that such gains are not sustained in elementary school. According to Dr. Whatley, "By the end of Kindergarten, the day care gains have washed out, though the children are on a par with other kindergarten children. The gains are wiped out by first grade. We don't know if they're picked up by third grade. We don't have enough data."

Given these findings, an effort is under way in the Comprehensive Child Day Care Program to coordinate the expanded day component better with the elementary school kindergarten: an hour a day of expanded day is set aside for children to do kindergarten homework, and expanded day curriculum emphasizes reinforcement of concepts learned in the kindergarten.

In addition, the Research and Evaluation unit is planning on using different instruments to measure differences in addition to cognitive gain, such as social adjustment.

The failure to sustain gains does not at all compromise the Title XX goals for the program, which are more specifically related to parental employment. However, it may raise questions for Atlanta's Board of Education, and for other school systems throughout the country that may want to justify any day care in educational terms rather than in broader social service terms.

THE PROGRAM MODEL AND PUBLIC SCHOOL CONTROL

The Comprehensive Child Day Care Program in Atlanta reflects both the strengths and some of the strains of a large public school system. While teachers feel that centralization of hiring and purchasing restricts their flexibility considerably, it also provides them stability and high pay and frees them from the continual fund-raising efforts of nonprofit centers that don't work through a system or confederation.

For parents using the program, one of the biggest advantages appears to be accessibility: i.e., the location of programs by school neighborhoods. As one parent says, "I could have put them in other day care centers, but I would have had to ride the bus. This was in the community. My other son was going to school here, so it was convenient. I spend a lot of time up here." This accessibility has increased the school attendance of children who might well otherwise be at home taking care of their younger brothers and sisters; one of the most noticeable features of the day care program is preschool-age children being escorted to and from school by their older brothers and sisters.

Actual parent involvement in the program, however, is somewhat limited. While a structure exists for parent participation in an advisory capacity for program planning and development, parents do not have a real stake in program survival, as they do in Brookline; perhaps implementation of the sliding-fee scale will change this somewhat. Involvement of parents in the program varies considerably from center to center, less as a function of administrative structure than of the personality of the teacher and school principal.

While the public schools now provide over 50 percent of all Title XX day care in Atlanta, no one I spoke to felt that expansion of day care in Atlanta should or could exclude either the private or the public sector. As one member of the Board of Education said, "Unless they let us use money for capital outlay, it would be too costly for the public schools to take over the whole system. Besides, I don't like to see the schools totally in charge of anything."

****

Education for Parenthood Pilot Project, Austin, Texas

SYNOPSIS

In a unique partnership, the Austin Independent School District (AISD) is teaming up with Child, Inc., Austin's largest private nonprofit day care agency, to offer day care to some 80 infants and toddlers.

Four high school-based Infant and Family Development Centers care for the children while their teen-aged parents attend school. In addition, the centers serve as laboratories for an Education for Parenthood Project which allows all high school students to learn about child growth and development.

Responsibility for all aspects of center operation—administration, staffing, financing, training—is shared between Child, Inc. and AISD in an unusual partnership. "We're personally very proud of this," says one AISD Assistant Superintendent, "though it wasn't easy to accomplish."

Child, Inc. Executive Director, James Strickland, adds good-humoredly, "People will see this isn't impossible; it's just almost impossible!"

SERVICE DATA

Extent of Service
Type and Number of
    Programs: 4 Laboratory Infant and Family Development Centers

Hours of Operation: 8 AM-4 PM during school year

Eligibility: Priority to children of school-age parents, but open to Austin community

Date Began Operating:	2 centers-September 1976; 2 centers-January 1977
Children Using Program:	72-80

Financing and Costs
Sources of Financing
FY 1977:

Texas Education Authority: $142,000
Department of Public Welfare (Title XX): $180,000
Child, Inc.: in-kind social and health services
AISD: constructed two modular facilities; in-kind administrative services

Costs:

Start up: approximately $1,000/child/month
Projected normal expenses: $242/child/month

Personnel

Only the Project Coordinator is an AISD employee; all others are officially employed by Child, Inc., though subject to supervision by the Project Coordinator.

HISTORY AND DEVELOPMENT

The major impetus for the Education for Parenthood Pilot Program and its infant care component was the dramatic incidence of teenage parenthood in Austin and Texas. In 1975, marriage and pregnancy were the third ranking cause of young women dropping out of Austin schools at age 16 or below. In the same year, teenage girls in Texas were giving birth at a rate five times that of all other women in the state; teenage marriage was increasing at a rate four times that of all Texans.

Like many other cities, Austin had been making some efforts to meet the needs of its school-age parents. Pregnant teenagers could transfer from any one of Austin's nine high schools to a special Teenage Parent Program, established in 1970. Throughout their pregnancies and until their babies were six weeks old, these Austin students could remain in a sheltered environment, continuing their academic studies and learning the fundamentals of child care. But if they wanted to remain in school after that, they had to transfer back to their original high schools and make child care arrangements on their own. After leaving the Teenage Parent Program, some 60 percent regularly dropped out of school.

"Our Teenage Parent Council saw that the program was inadequate," says Mrs. Larue Allison, Head of Home Economics Education in the Austin Public Schools. "They wanted to develop a program that would provide care for the children and do teaching."

With the initiative of Mrs. Allison, cooperation from many Austin agencies, and three years' worth of pilot funding from the Texas Education Agency, the Austin School District is now sponsoring an Education for Parenthood program that includes, as one of its components, laboratory Infant and Family Development Centers (infant day care) at four of its high schools.

Aside from allowing school-age parents to complete their education, explicit goals of the program include preparing students for work in the child care field and for the "responsibilities of parenthood" (including, as the statement of program objectives puts it, for "the disadvantages of having children before they are able to care for, support, and enjoy [them]").

Even though the Education for Parenthood program provides care from 8 AM until 4 PM, AISD administrators emphasize that they are "not in the day care business." According to AISD's director of Career Education, "In all our vocational programs we think the best approach is hands-on experience. It's one thing to tell a student that changing babies is messy; it's another to actually change one. Likewise, if we're going to teach them about parenthood, we should provide infants; the logical infants are those of teenage parents. . . . But we're not in the infant care business. If we were, if I had started with Shanker's position, this would never have gotten out of my office."

Who, then, does have responsibility for providing child care?

Actually, responsibility is shared between the Austin Schools and Child, Inc., Austin's largest nonprofit child care agency, which operates twenty day care centers for children aged three to five, three infant-toddler centers for children age six weeks to three years, as well as Home Start and family day care homes.

The development of this unusual cooperative venture between a private agency and a public school system is complicated, to say the least. When initially contacted about the laboratory infant centers, Child, Inc. agreed to do anything it could to help, from the most low-key consulting role to all-out operation of the program. According to Child, Inc. Executive Director James Strickland, "The original objective was not to do the program in a specific way. It was to see how best we could coordinate the program. If we had a set way in mind, it probably couldn't have been done. The program developed a life of its own."

Revisions in program design were constantly made, with an overall effect that was dramatic. To obviate the need for new facilities, for example, original plans called for the laboratory component of the program to operate in Child, Inc. day care centers, with staff provided by the Austin Public Schools. But travel time between these centers and most of Austin's high schools was too great. In final form, the program operates out of public school facilities—including two pre-fab units built especially for the project—and is staffed by Child, Inc. employees.

Among many obstacles to program development were the objections of several high school principals. "I don't want those pregnant girls on my campus," said one. Another principal from a Mexican-American neighborhood, who reluctantly agreed to accommodate an infant care center, now reflects, "Initially I had reservations about whether I wanted the lab on the campus. I asked myself, 'Do I really want a program that appears to be condoning this type of activity?' But after waiting so long for the lab to open and then seeing what happens when these girls are given another opportunity to graduate from high school, I believe I did the right thing." (Project statistics bear out the effectiveness of the program in keeping teenage parents in school: with the availability of infant care, the dropout rate has fallen from 60 percent to some 15 percent.)

Still, it is hard to combat the mistaken notion that the program is promoting teenage pregnancy. "Because the child care labs get all the publicity," says one Austin official, "people think of this only as a day care program. What isn't recognized is the parenthood education." Moreover, conservative opponents of the program have erroneously linked it with "sex education," a confusion that will no doubt plague other communities trying to initiate education for parenthood programs. Growing cautious about the purposes of the pilot project it was sponsoring, and saying that it wanted to fund only the "educational component and not social services," the Texas Education Authority reduced the second year of pilot funding from a requested $232,000 to $133,719.

Even without any further cuts in TEA funds, the program is only eligible for one more year of pilot funding; so the real test for the viability of this public school-private agency partnership will come in 1979, at the latest.

Administrators in both agencies think it unlikely that AISD will pick up the entire costs of the program, especially the costs of the day care component. According to AISD Assistant Superintendent Kay Killough, "At this point in time, the Superintendent's cabinet prefers that the provision of day care not be the district's responsibility. And there are some good reasons for that, politically as well as financially. It's not in the state's funding pattern, though I'm not sure this will always be the case."

Child, Inc.'s James Strickland is even less optimistic about public school financing of day care, in Texas or anywhere else: "I don't think the electorate will stand for the public school system taking responsibility for younger children because of what it will cost. That's my basic argument with Shanker's plan—it won't work. People are running for local office on the platform of 'no more taxes.' "

To both administrators, the precariousness of continued funding highlights the advantages of the public school partnership with a private agency. According to Killough, "If local money is not available, we have an agency to continue the child care portion of the program so that we can continue the educational components." And according to Strickland, "Private non-profit agencies have a lot to offer public schools in nurturing these programs. The schools would be told to raise their tax base. We can avoid that by tapping into alternative funding sources, as well as getting some city tax money through the city council."

While the Austin City Council does donate local tax funds as a matching share for Title XX, its contribution—some $240,000 in FY 1977—does not generate enough support to meet Austin's day care need. Moreover, while most parents enrolled in the Education for Parenthood program are eligible for subsidy under Title XX, a significant number are not. And so a key question for Austin becomes: can it maintain a program with the open eligibility that is a major characteristic and advantage of the public schools?

State legislation providing for funding of Education for Parenthood and day care programs in nine Texas school districts has been introduced by state representative Wilhelmina Delco, former chairperson of the Austin Board of Education. However, given legislative concern for costs of education in general, its passage is doubtful.

More promising, perhaps, is the plan of James Strickland to change the Title XX criteria. "By the time this pilot funding ends, I'm hoping we'll have the Title XX eligibility criteria changed. A slight expansion could include the 'at risk' population, which children of teenage parents would be."

Even if the Title XX criteria are not changed, project's end will find four new well-functioning infant centers, two of them in facilities built and owned by the Austin Public Schools. They can be leased to Child, Inc., which can operate them for use by those children of teenage parents who do qualify for Title XX, teenage parents who otherwise might well have had to drop out of school.

Perhaps even more important for Austin, and for the rest of the country, is that the potential strength of the public school-private agency partnership will have been demonstrated.

ADMINISTRATIVE STRUCTURE

The administrative structure for Austin's infant care centers is a hybrid, the result of a cross between two institutions that differ notably.

AISD serves some 60,000 primary and secondary students; its teaching personnel must be certified according to district and state requirements and are hired by the administrators without any parent involvement; its superintendent and other administrators are ultimately responsible to an elected school board.

Child, Inc. is a nonprofit agency providing child care to some 1,800 children under the age of five; it encourages the employment of community people, requiring minimal educational qualifications and relying heavily on parent participation in the hiring of staff; its executive director is responsible to a board composed largely of parents with children in its programs and with an equivalent racial distribution among blacks, Chicanos, and Anglos.

The full Education for Parenthood Program operates under the auspices of the School District, and is administered by its Career Development Department, in close cooperation with the Department of Home Economics. However, responsibility for operation of the laboratory infant centers which are at the heart of the program is shared between the School District and Child, Inc. This partnership administrative structure affects virtually every aspect of program operation, bringing with it both strengths and strains.

"Indeed we do have problems in meshing two large bureaucracies," says Child, Inc. Executive Director Strickland. "To the point of saying—on both sides—we could do this more efficiently, easily, with less strain, if we did it ourselves. But the question on both sides is 'would it be as beneficial to the community if we did it alone?' And the answer on both sides is 'no.' Yes it's a hassle, yes it's frustrating, but the end result wouldn't be as good."

At the time of this writing, Child, Inc. and AISD were still working out the detailed administrative procedures. Rather than dwelling on complexities, this section will highlight some key administrative issues:

1) System-wide Administration: The Partnership Model
2) On-site Administration
3) Strengths and Strains of the Partnership Structure

System-wide Administration: The Partnership Model

As the accompanying organizational chart indicates, two separate administrative systems, operating in tandem, have responsibility for the laboratory child care component of the Parenthood Education Program.

As part of AISD, the program is administered directly by the Department of Career Development, which includes the Department of Home Economics. Major on-line responsibility for program development rests with a Program Coordinator, hired by Career Development with input from Home Economics. The Program Coordinator oversees the director of each infant care center, and maintains major contact with Child, Inc. through its executive director.

As part of Child, Inc., the program is overseen by the Child, Inc. Executive Director. The director of infant care for Child, Inc.—along with the Program Coordinator for AISD—is in charge of all hiring and training.

The most frequent interface between the two programs in terms of day-to-day operation is between the AISD Program Coordinator and the Child, Inc. Executive Director. They make the day-to-day decisions for program development.

All major policy decisions are made jointly by the Child, Inc. Executive Director—acting on the advice of his Board of Directors—and the AISD Director of Career Development, acting on behalf of the AISD Superintendent and/or Assistant Superintendent.

On-site Administration

Since they operate on or adjacent to high school campuses, final on-site responsibility for the programs rests with the school principal.
In effect, however, it is center directors who are responsible for day to day operation.

Center directors are official employees of Child, Inc. However, since they also are supervised by the AISD Program Coordinator, directors must work within two administrative frameworks. Or, as one director put it, "I have two bosses."

On the AISD side, center directors report directly to the program coordinator for the Parenthood Education Project. They also coordinate their daily activities with Career Development and Home Economics staff in the high schools, whose students work or observe at the centers.

Since the teachers in their centers are officially employees of Child, Inc., center directors also work closely with the Child, Inc. Infant Care Director, who is responsible for much staff training.

Smooth functioning at the center level of this administrative hybrid depends to a great extent on clear lines of communication between the AISD Program Coordinator and representatives of Child, Inc.

Strengths and Strains of the Partnership Structure

Shared administrative responsibility for one program brings with it inevitable strengths and strains.

According to the AISD's Director of Career Development, "The real strength is that we've been able to focus two administrative structures on the solution of a common need. The problems are two in nature. We interface so closely that some of my staff don't know who they're working for. The other problem is that we're trying very hard not to develop territorial needs that cannot be met."

To a great extent, the program's uniqueness derives from the fact that it doesn't exist squarely within either AISD or Child, Inc. territory, that it

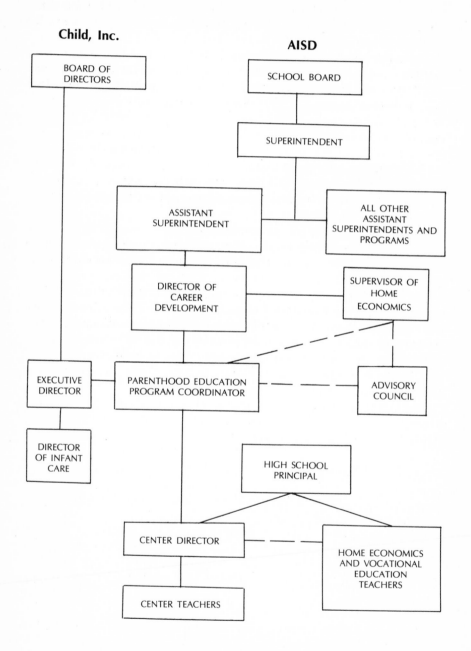

ADMINISTRATION, AUSTIN

Child, Inc.

BOARD OF
DIRECTORS

AISD

SCHOOL BOARD

SUPERINTENDENT

ASSISTANT
SUPERINTENDENT

ALL OTHER
ASSISTANT
SUPERINTENDENTS AND
PROGRAMS

DIRECTOR OF
CAREER
DEVELOPMENT

SUPERVISOR OF
HOME
ECONOMICS

EXECUTIVE
DIRECTOR

PARENTHOOD EDUCATION
PROGRAM COORDINATOR

ADVISORY
COUNCIL

DIRECTOR
OF INFANT
CARE

HIGH SCHOOL
PRINCIPAL

CENTER DIRECTOR

HOME ECONOMICS
AND VOCATIONAL
EDUCATION
TEACHERS

CENTER TEACHERS

rests somewhere between and therefore avoids the standard operating procedure of each institution. In certain areas, such as staff training, this brings advantages to both participants. Because it is somewhat different from other Child, Inc. infant care programs, training has been specially designed to draw on both the in-house resources at Child, Inc. and the resources available through the School District.

Other aspects of the partnership prove more advantageous for one group than the other. For example, both staff qualifications and the pay scale for this special program fall between those normally used by each of the agencies (higher than Child, Inc.'s, lower than AISD's). This arrangement provides a beneficial precedent for Child, Inc. to upgrade its entire pay scale and to increase requisite staff qualifications. However, if they are being paid well by Child, Inc. standards, center directors feel that they should be on the full AISD scale, especially since much of their job entails the supervision of high school students who are observing or working in the laboratory centers.

The uniqueness of the program creates one other important administrative strain: heavy reliance on constant communication between Child, Inc.'s Executive Director and the AISD's Program Coordinator, the key figures in each of the two cooperating agencies. As the latter says, "We have a real problem when both of us are out of town at the same time."

Commenting on the entire administrative structure, James Strickland says, "We are slowly working out procedures to make this work; after problems, we back up and say, 'how did we mess that up?' It takes a real commitment to an unclear potential, to something we think is going to be better than what's going on."

FINANCING AND COSTS

Financing

Infant day care provided as part of the Education for Parenthood program is financed largely by pilot grants from the Texas Education Authority (TEA), most of which is then used to leverage Title XX monies. Both AISD and Child, Inc. also make significant in-kind contributions, though these are not used as a matching share for Title XX funds. There are no parent fees involved yet in support of the program; Texas has no sliding-fee scale for Title XX.

Total project costs during FY 1976, the first year of operation, were approximately $329,000 plus in-kind contributions. Sources of funds were:

TEA: $142,000

Department of Public
    Welfare (Title XX): $180,000

Child, Inc.: $7,000 subsidy of net operating loss, plus
                              in-kind contribution of social services and
                              health staff

AISD: In-kind contribution of administrative staff
                              who managed the grant and of home
                              economics staff; contributions of two
                              facilities, with cost to be refinanced
                              through lease to Child, Inc.: no cash
                              expenditure beyond regular school
                              budget.

     The following diagram depicts the flow of TEA funds through the various agencies and to the project. In 1976-77, AISD received $142,379 from TEA. It then subcontracted to Child, Inc. for purchase of service in the amount of $97,188. Child, Inc., in turn, was able to use some $60,000 of this as a donated funds contribution to Title XX, generating an additional $180,000 under the 3 for 1 matching formula. Even with this, the heavy cost of start-up meant a net loss to Child, Inc. of approximately $7,000 during the first year of operation.

Flow Through

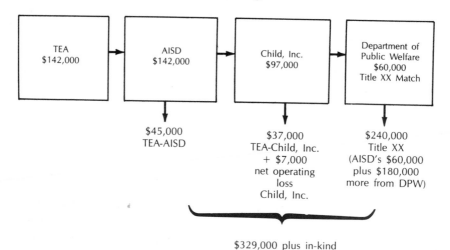

Sources of Funds for the AISD Education for Parenthood Project

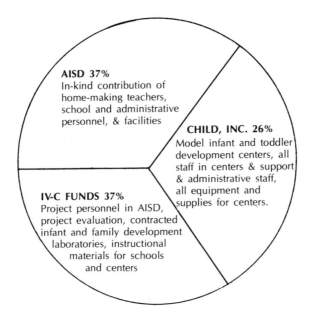

AISD 37%
In-kind contribution of home-making teachers, school and administrative personnel, & facilities

CHILD, INC. 26%
Model infant and toddler development centers, all staff in centers & support & administrative staff, all equipment and supplies for centers.

IV-C FUNDS 37%
Project personnel in AISD, project evaluation, contracted infant and family development laboratories, instructional materials for schools and centers

Costs

There are two cost dimensions for this project: the cost of infant care and the cost of participation by high school students in the educational component of the program, which includes a "hands on" laboratory experience.

Available cost data is for the start-up phase of the program, when the costs of direct caregiving are therefore considerably higher than they would be after all program elements are in place and after full enrollment has been achieved. Average starting cost per child for an eight-hour day has been figured at $250/week. Average starting cost for AISD high school students has been figured at $47 per academic quarter; ongoing costs are projected at $15 per quarter.

Projected costs of infant care during the second year of operation are $242 per month, or one-fourth the costs of the first year. Infant care in Child, Inc. programs not affiliated with AISD will cost slightly more, $250 per month. Cost savings will be realized because some AISD student-trainees will be used as teacher aides in the infant centers, and because the cost of renting the laboratory facilities from AISD is lower than other Child, Inc. rentals.

ELIGIBILITY

Eligibility for use of the laboratory infant centers is open to the entire Austin Community. However, a set of provisional priorities for enrollment have been established by the Advisory Council to the Parenthood Education Project.

Priorities and requirements for eligibility are as follows:

1) High school students with a child

Most parents using the program are high school students. All are females, though the program does not exclude fathers. To use the centers, students must apply to Child, Inc. and they must enroll in at least one Education for Parenthood course in their high school. Students can transfer from one high school to another in order to enroll their children in the laboratory centers.

Most but not all student-parents are eligible for child care subsidy under Title XX. The fees of those who are not Title XX eligible are subsidized by AISD with TEA funds for the pilot program.

2) Non-high school Child, Inc. families

Second priority is given to families who have already applied to or who have children enrolled in a Child, Inc. program. Parents in this category are not high school students and are not eligible for Parenthood Education courses.

3) Non-high school, non-Child, Inc. families

Families in this category have neither a student-parent nor a child already enrolled in, or on the waiting list of, another Child, Inc. program. They include families eligible for and not eligible for Title XX, including those in which one parent is an employee of the School District.

While these requirements allow for participation by all members of the Austin community, most users of the program are Title XX eligible high school parents. Out of some 80 slots available in September 1977, 60 were occupied by children of AISD students and the rest by Child, Inc. Title XX families. It is unlikely that the program will enroll many, if any, children of parents who are neither attending high school nor eligible for Title XX; such parents must pay full program costs, including costs of social services, whether they need them or not.

PERSONNEL

The hybrid nature of the Education for Parenthood project is reflected in all of its staffing policies and procedures.

Child, Inc. and AISD differ significantly in their employment policies. A community-based agency with a parent-controlled board, Child, Inc. puts a premium on experience and on racial diversity, rather than credentials; of its 246 staff members, 115 are black, 83 Chicano, and 47 Anglo. Like most school districts, AISD puts a premium on professional certification and pays its teachers more than day care workers; most of AISD's employees are anglo.

Personnel policies for the laboratory infant centers fall between rather than squarely within either the AISD or the Child, Inc. framework.

Criteria

The difference in qualifications required to work in Child, Inc. and AISD programs is substantial. Child, Inc. requires that its staff earn the G.E.D. within a "certain period of time." As James Strickland says, "we have a lot of people who don't have a high school education, but they're dynamic with children. We want to give them a chance." While Child, Inc. prefers college degrees in early childhood education for its teachers, and requires them of its infant center directors, it does not hold fast to these criteria. "We are working towards degreed people; the problem is the salary—we can't attract degreed people."

The Austin Public Schools, by contrast, absolutely require college degrees. To direct the laboratory nursery school at Austin High School, for example—the position most comparable to directing one of the infant care centers—a vocational B.A. with homemaking certification is required. AISD insisted that degreed people direct the centers sponsored under the Education for Parenthood program.

The agreement worked out to staff the laboratory infant centers is more in line with AISD criteria, even though all staff members are officially employed by Child, Inc. Directors are required to have a vocational bachelor's, if not a master's, degree in homemaking with an emphasis on child and family development. Other staff members—teachers and caregivers—are required to have college or high school degrees, respectively.

Child, Inc.'s Strickland views this agreement not as a threat to community people but as a welcome opportunity to upgrade qualifications within his agency. "The qualifications required of preschool teachers have been abysmal—there was an overreaction to degrees in the 1960's. I don't think we need a pendulum reaction to more degrees, but we do need some normalization. If we have a chance to upgrade qualifications—and that's what the AISD program gives us—we can also upgrade salaries, because they require more credentials."

Salaries

Salaries in the laboratory infant centers are a compromise between Child, Inc. and AISD salary schedules.

Center directors start at $10,270 for a 12-month year, considerably more than the $8,000 to $9,000 per full year earned by directors at other Child, Inc. centers but less than the beginning salary of high school home economics teachers ($9,500 for a nine-month academic year). Laboratory center teachers start at $7,200, compared to the $6,916 earned initially by teachers in other Child, Inc. centers.

With pay higher than the regular Child, Inc. scale and lower than the AISD scale, employees of the hybrid program find themselves in an awkward position. "Naturally there is some resentment by my regular infant care staff of the higher salaries in the AISD program," says Child, Inc.'s James Strickland. "But I see this as an attempt to upgrade the salary schedules of all Child, Inc. employees; if we can get away with this, we can begin to raise the whole system."

On the other hand, employees of the special program tend to feel that they are being underpaid, that they should be earning on a par with high school home economics teachers. As one center director explains, "We're responsible for training and evaluating high school students. Sometimes we take over the high school class. These aren't responsibilities that Child, Inc. employees have—and we have higher credentials."

Salary ranges for the different programs are:

	AISD Teachers	*Child, Inc.*
B.A.	$ 9,500 - $15,052 in 14 steps	$ 6,916 - $10,210 in 9 steps
M.A.	$10,449 - $16,557 in 16 steps	

Hiring Procedures

Child, Inc. receives all applications for work in its infant centers, including the Education for Parenthood laboratory centers. It passes the applications along to special review committees which include representatives of both Child, Inc. and AISD.

Teacher and caregiver applications are reviewed by a committee composed of the AISD Program Coordinator, Child, Inc. Infant Center Director, and a director of one of the laboratory infant centers.

Applications to direct one of the infant centers are screened by the AISD Program Coordinator, Child, Inc. Infant Center Director, Child, Inc. Personnel Director, and the AISD Coordinator of Home Economics.

Although parents usually sit on screening committees for other Child, Inc. applicants, no parents review personnel for positions in the laboratory infant centers.

OPERATIONAL ISSUES: LABORATORY USE

Unlike other programs profiled in this report, the primary—or at least ostensible—purpose of the infant centers is to provide a laboratory situation in which high school students can prepare for parenthood or for work with young children.

High school students have a variety of experiences at, or in connection with, the laboratories. Education for Parenthood participants are trained to understand child growth and development through direct observation and interaction, and by filling out daily pattern sheets, which are kept to chart individual behavioral patterns and developmental milestones. Home economics students in sewing make curtains and other materials for the centers, while those in food management study the nutritional needs of young children.

Overall use of the program has been greater than expected. Original program plans anticipated use of the laboratories by approximately 100 vocational education students in what the Austin schools call a Pre-employment Learning Experience (PLE), and by some 1800 home economics students taking child development or education for parenthood courses. Project tallies for 1976-77 reveal that 60 PLE students (one male, 59 females) and 1982 education for parenthood students (433 male, 1549 female) have used the program.

Not included in any official program planning are the number of students enrolled in neither educational track who use their lunch-hours to observe the infants in the laboratory centers. The infant labs have been so popular that the only one in a church—without an observation booth—had to put a limit on the number of student visits.

PARENT INVOLVEMENT

There are considerable differences in the roles played by parents in most Child, Inc. and AISD programs. Child, Inc. prides itself on a parent board which makes all major policy decisions and on personnel committees (often ad hoc) which usually include parents in the hiring of staff.

AISD, by contrast, has an elected school board which sets policy; it does not include parents in the hiring of personnel.

Parent involvement in the Education for Parenthood program is closer to the AISD than to the Child, Inc. model. As James Strickland explains, "There was little parent involvement in organizing this. This program was pretty much set in concrete before it was presented to the Board; and there was little if any resistance to the fact that they hadn't been involved. Our parents are astute enough to know that they'd be able to change something they don't like. This board is very well informed in the area of what alternatives they have in terms of developing programs with the public schools. They know the battle that's being built nationally between public schools and some preschool programs; they're proud that they can build a model of cooperation."

The board members Strickland speaks of include no teenage parents, and no direct users of the Education for Parenthood program. Admittedly "timid and shy" about board membership and policy decisions, teenage parents are involved, in a number of ways, in the daily life of the program.

Parent involvement in the infant centers is structured—and required—in three ways. All student parents who enroll children in the infant centers must take courses in Education for Parenthood (at least one a year, and possibly one per quarter). In addition, class time is set aside for "Mother's Clubs" or meetings of all the parents, so that all parents of children in each center can be together on a regular basis to share their concerns. At least one principal, who encouraged this type of parental visitation, is trying to arrange for academic credit for the teenage parents to be with their children. Moreover, parents who use the centers are required to fill out daily "pattern sheets" when they arrive and to bring them home at the end of the day; the pattern sheets provide a structured format for parents to record their observations about their children at home and to share them with staff, and for staff to share with parents their observations of what the infants did during the day at the center.

There are two other types of unstructured involvement. For one, most student parents spend time in the center at the beginning of the day, when they drop their children off; and they return at lunchtime, to observe or to visit with their infants. Second, many student parents are also signed up in the pre-employment infant care program, and get to spend additional time doing "field work" with their own children. One student explains that being a student and being a mother does not create a conflict for her: "I can do things here that I can't do at home. She likes to do a lot of things here. I try to let her do a lot of things home she does here. She's real smart."

The involvement that AISD has been concerned about in implementing the program is keeping students in school after they became parents.

Looked at this way, "involvement" seems high: the drop-out rate may be reduced from 60 percent all the way down to 15 percent. As one student says, "Before they had this up I was really missing a lot of days . . . if someone in my family wasn't available, I'd just stay at home."

MONITORING AND EVALUATION

As a grantee of the TEA, the Education for Parenthood Project is monitored by TEA staff. In addition, the project includes an independent evaluation by an Austin-based consulting firm, ARBEC.

PROGRAM MODEL AND PUBLIC SCHOOL CONTROL

The infant and Family Development Centers of the Education for Parenthood Project offer a promising model of public-private partnership for meeting the needs of a special population (teenage parents) or others in need of child care.

Public school financing of two facilities, as well as receipt of pilot funding from the Texas Education Authority, make it possible for Child, Inc. to expand the population of infants and toddlers it was already serving. Child, Inc. access to Title XX dollars and, perhaps to other non-school-tax related dollars, provide a possible basis for continuity of the project.

As in Atlanta, no one I spoke with in Austin felt that expansion of day care should exclude either the public or private sector. Perhaps because they were on their way to developing a strong partnership model, the strongest commitment was to "whatever will work."

****

Family Day Care in Anderson 5 and Pickens County, South Carolina

SYNOPSIS

With 20 of its 92 school districts operating day care programs, South Carolina has the most extensive system of school-based day care of any state except California. More important here, however, is the existence in South Carolina of two school-affiliated family day care programs, probably the first in the nation. In Anderson 5, a suburban school district in the western part of the state, a small family day care program takes care of infants through five-year-olds as an extension of the district's center-based programs. In the most rural north-western School District of Pickens

County, family day care supplements kindergarten for five-year-olds, and meets the needs of working parents for a full day of child care.

This profile will highlight South Carolina's public school family day care programs, placing them in the broader context of day care delivery in the state.

SERVICE DATA

State Department of Education Child Development Programs

	State Funded CD Centers	*ARC Funded CD Centers*
Number and Type:	14 of 92 school districts	5 school districts
	35 centers for children aged 3-5	11 centers for children aged 3-5
	46 extended day for five year olds	46 extended day for five year olds
Hours of Operation:	8 AM to 5 PM during school year	7 AM to 6 PM center care for 12 months
		8 AM to 3 PM extended day only during school year
Children:	2,580 total in 1976-77	
Financing:	Mixture of financing varies from school district to school district; includes Title XX, ARC funds, certified public expenditures, and some direct cash expenditures by school districts.	
Cost per Child:	3 and 4 year olds - $985/year. Kindergarten extended day - $788	
Personnel:	All staff are employees of the local school district. Teachers working in center-based programs must meet school district certification requirements. Family day care providers do not need formal educational certification, but must be screened by both the school district personnel and the licensing agent from DSS.	

Family Day Care

	Anderson 5	*Pickens County*
Number Family Day Care Homes:	8 - 10	7

Hours of Operation:	7 AM - 6 PM year round	8 AM - 4 PM in two half-day shifts, school year
Children Served:	Ages 0 - 3, approximately 38 per year, up to six per home depending upon age	Age five (kindergarten) approximately 40 per year, four or five per home
Financing:	ARC Title XX Parent Fees	ARC School District Cash and In-kind
Total Program Costs:	$80,000-$95,000 per 12-month year	$27,000-$77,000 per 9-month school year $1,100 per child per school year
Personnel:	Public school employees Salary Range: $4,420-$6,760 per year	Public school employees Salary Range: $3,600-$4,000 per school year

HISTORY AND DEVELOPMENT

South Carolina

Although the development of public school affiliated day care in South Carolina is relatively recent—it dates to 1971—it is more widespread than in any other state except California.

Prior to 1971, there was little publicly funded day care in South Carolina; slow to participate in the Title IV-A funding process, the state funded only one program through its Department of Social Services.

In 1971, however, two sources of funds became available that required no matching share from the state. Early in the year, approximately $1.5 million of ARC funds became available—the first year of a five-year funding cycle—to those six northwestern counties of the state that fell into the Appalachian Regional Commission area. And in the fall of 1971, with passage of national child development legislation looking imminent, non-ARC areas became eligible for some $2 million of Emergency Employment Funds allocated by then Governor West for the establishment of child care centers.

Governor West's initiative came two years after the South Carolina legislature approved a ten-year plan for state financing of kindergarten. (A 1968 Moody Investor's Report on the state's financial health recommended the extension of public school down to age five, because of the large number of "culturally deprived children.") As we shall see, the development and future of public school-based day care in South Carolina has been intricately related to the development of the kindergarten program.

For implementation of both ARC-funded and EEA-funded day care programs, the state looked to the public schools, creating what might now be called a "presumed prime sponsorship." Local school districts were given first crack at sponsoring and operating day care; if they were unable or unwilling to do so, other agencies would be considered.

"The primary reason the schools were approached," according to Joel Taylor, Chief of School Services in the State Department of Education, "is that they had vacant buildings and the management capability; they didn't have to rent facilities." Indeed, EEA funding covered the costs of personnel but not facilities. Moreover, to take advantage of EEA funds, it was important to have an agency or system that could gear up quickly. According to South Carolina Deputy Superintendent for Instruction, Dr. Charlie Williams, "The public schools were the most readily accessible and economical delivery model."

In the ARC area, "presumed prime sponsorship" met with little, if any, opposition. According to Ms. Jackie Oakley, a regional coordinator for the Appalachian Regional Commission, "Opposition to the public school was never an issue. At that time, public schools were the only ones interested in it. Five years ago you didn't have everybody wanting child development dollars; now you've got five requests for every dollar, from CAP agencies, Y's, private-for-profit groups, Head Starts, hospitals, technical centers, etc."

A few South Carolina school districts, where the superintendent took the initiative, jumped at the chance of funding. But overall, in both ARC and non-ARC areas, public schools did not exactly come running to sponsor child care programs. In some areas they became the sponsoring agency more or less by default; they were the only available agency that could operate a program without constructing new facilities.

There were many reasons for the reluctance of school districts to get involved in child care programs. According to Jackie Oakley, "Most of the time they felt they had enough trouble trying to meet the needs of 6-18 year olds. And five years ago, child care was still a pretty new idea down here; we were just getting going into the integration process full force. Also, schools didn't want to have to deal with the licensing agencies, the FIDCR requirements, and all that." Even more important for non-ARC school districts was the lack of assurance that the programs would be continued after the two years of EEA funding ran out.

In the Appalachian area, six of 16 school districts in the six county area took advantage of ARC funds, opening 13 child development centers that have served approximately 1,100 children. In non-ARC areas, 14 of 92 school districts took advantage of the EEA funds; 20 centers were opened, serving approximately 2,000 children. (Where school districts did not participate, EEA funds were contracted for with the Department of Social Services.)

Every year since 1973, when EEA funding ran out, the South Carolina legislature has appropriated approximately $1 million for continuation of the child development programs. But during this same period, South Carolina has also been expanding its state supported kindergarten program, increasing appropriations from $500,000 in 1969 to $7,242,120 in 1976-77. With some 25 percent of the eligible kindergarten population still to be served, state policy-makers find themselves in a squeeze to justify expenditures on a program for preschoolers that originally started with EEA funds, when there are still five-year-olds not being served by kindergarten.

The State Department of Education has clearly put top priority on completing its kindergarten program. (Among its objectives for 1980, adopted by the state Board in January 1977, is to provide a statewide public kindergarten to all five-year-old children in South Carolina by 1978.) Ironically, however, achievement of a statewide kindergarten program may hinge on continuation of child care programs. Planners in the department of education have found that many parents don't or can't take advantage of the free kindergarten because it only operates for three hours in the morning or the afternoon. According to Joel Taylor, "The reality we're facing is the working parent. That's the most critical one."

Some school districts are already trying to achieve their target kindergarten enrollments by offering full-day sessions. Two districts are using their state child development appropriation to serve five-year-olds instead of three- and four-year-olds in a child care center. And one rural district, to be profiled more extensively in this report, has developed a family day care program to work in conjunction with its kindergarten. Children spend one half-day in kindergarten and the other half-day in a family day care home; many of these children might otherwise be at home alone or under the supervision of siblings.

Whether or not the public schools will be able to continue providing day care in South Carolina is doubtful, or, at best, problematic. Most ARC funding—which has been used as a match for Title XX—will run out by the late 1970s. Local tax revenues for education in South Carolina, like everywhere else, are harder and harder to come by. And there is little indication that the state legislature will expand its child development appropriation before kindergarten becomes available to all South Carolina five-year-olds.

"It's all a matter of funds," says Joel Taylor. "If we had the money, we've proved we can do the job. Administratively, we've proven that school districts can operate full day care."

In the absence of adequate funding, the state Department of Education is moving to implement, by 1980, "parent-oriented education programs for early childhood development." "A public supported system of institutionalized day care centers in the public schools seems to be sometime in the future," says Taylor. "But we're still committed to early learning. If the school system can find some means to assist children—by t.v., media, whatever—at least we will be continuing the effort." In 1977-78, 150 elementary schools will offer classes for parents of children under age six in topics such as "how and what your child learns through play" and "how your child learns to read." According to Ms. Marjorie Sparrow, Program Coordinator, "It's an attempt to make parents aware of the importance of their role in the total development of their children, with an emphasis on home activities and everyday parenting skills."

But what if money were available in South Carolina to implement a broad-scale day care program? A household survey of the Appalachian Regional area conducted in 1974 by the South Carolina Office of Child Development revealed that most consumers and potential consumers of child care wanted it to be affiliated with a major societal institution, such as the public school or a church. However, according to Ms. Betty Carnes, Director of the Office of Child Development in the Department of Social Services, the state's major provider of publicly funded day care, "It should be left up to the local community. In some areas the school is the only one; in others, it wouldn't work at all. I would oppose prime sponsorship being given to any one agency."

State Superintendent of Education Dr. Cyril Busbee seems to agree: "I am not at all sure that the public school is the agency to provide child care for children from six weeks old on to age five. I'm open to persuasion; they may well be. But the public school as an institution can't do everything for everybody at all ages."

Family Day Care in Anderson 5

Among the first school districts in South Carolina to provide day care was Anderson 5, which serves the city of Anderson. District Superintendent William B. Royster came to Anderson with a doctorate from the University of Maryland's Institute for Child Study and with a firm belief in the advantages of early intervention. "What affects one area of a child's life affects all others. We have to break into the cycle somewhere. The earlier you do, the better off you are." As early as 1970, Royster tried to interest the state Department of Education in taking advantage of Title IV-A programs to develop programs for young children; but at that time, the department was preoccupied with the beginnings of the statewide kindergarten program.

In 1972, the availability of ARC funds as the matching share for Title IV-A enabled Anderson to launch two child development programs. A former elementary school was converted into a Child Development Center for children aged three to five. Those preschoolers unable to attend the Center could participate in a Home-Based program which sent professionals and paraprofessionals into their homes. Enrollment in these programs has fluctuated with the availability of funding and shifts in federal and state eligibility criteria, but at its peak in 1972-73, the Child Development Center was serving some 350 children. Before its ARC funding expired in March 1977, the Home-Based program was serving some 100 children, representing a sharp decline from the original population of 250 in 1972-73.

Neither the Center nor the Home-Based program, however, met the day care needs of families with children under three. Nor did any other agency in the country. "Mothers were desperate for child care for infants and children under three," says the Child Development Center's social worker. "And they needed the child care now, not next week, because the jobs were now. Anderson is a textile area, and people have to show up or lose their work." So, in August 1975, using ARC dollars as a match for Title XX funds provided by the Department of Social Services, Anderson 5 became the first school district in South Carolina—and probably in the country—to offer family day care.

At any one time, the school district operates from eight to ten family day care homes spread throughout rural Anderson County, each serving an average of four children. According to licensing law, family day care homes can serve up to six children, including the provider's own children aged sixteen or below. As public school employees, family day care providers are paid a basic wage of $40 per week plus $15 for each child, and are entitled to such benefits as health and life insurance. Moreover, they receive a stock of equipment and supplies—rocking horse, Creative Playthings sink, baby carriage, easel and paints, crayons, scissors, paste, etc.—as well as back-up support and supervision from the school district's Family Day Care Coordinator.

During its first two years of operation (August 1975-August 1977), the program employed some 30 family day care providers. The high rate of turnover is accounted for largely because the original plan worked out by the Anderson 5 school district and the Department of Social Services, the major funder of the program, stipulated that providers would be employed by the public school for only one year. After that "training period," they would be on their own. As Anderson 5's family day care coordinator explains it, "This is a big rural county with a great need for day care. The government is spending money to train people to get satellite homes going. If you hire eight people for five years, you haven't reached the community. The government is really spending money to train people to get satellite homes going. Those who aren't going to keep at it weed themselves out anyway."

"The goal was really to demonstrate that family day care was viable in South Carolina," according to one school official. However, after their "training period" as school employees is over, many providers cannot maintain their public school income unless they charge more, take in more children, or both. "I'll probably continue on my own," says one, looking ahead, "but most won't. If you do day care on your own, you have to charge more than mothers can pay. Day care on your own, which I've done before, means spending almost everything you take in on equipment and food." Says another, "Now they're paying eight or nine dollars a week. I told them I'll have to charge more, between $15 and $18, and I'd have to get two more kids. The increase will hurt them too; they're all on such a tight budget. But they're all so pleased. I'll see how many I can tend to. I won't overload myself with children. I want to try to keep it around six to eight children." But there are many families, most of them funded through Title XX, who will not be able to continue their family day care arrangements; as one provider says, "It would be hard for them to even pay $10 a week." (And under Title XX guidelines, any client paying a fee will lose eligibility certification.)

Termination as public school employees also means the loss of the supportive services of the program's family day care coordinator. "I call her whenever I have a problem," says one provider. "She calls me once or sometimes twice a week. If there's a speaker or training of any kind, she lets me know and we make arrangements to go. She gives me transportation . . . And if you have a problem with a parent, it's just easy to say 'the center says.' I had one father who said he would be late now and then; I said 'this is the time the center says.' It's easier when you have someone behind you . . . I like having somebody to turn to when I have a problem. I've been in day care a long time and I know a lot, but I don't know everything."

After two years, project records indicate that only one of 30 providers has maintained her day care home independent of the public school subsidy, and she has expanded to offer "group home" services for some 15 to 20 children. Given the failure to build a network of satellite family day care homes and, in many cases, the disruption of the bond between caregiver and child just after it had been established, DSS agreed in summer 1977 to allow Anderson 5 to employ its family day care staff for up to two years.

Whether or not Anderson 5's family day care program will last beyond its third year is largely a matter of matching funds. "The people are there if the money is there," says Diane Earl, the program coordinator. ARC funds, appropriated on a five-year funding cycle, are due to expire in June 1980, but the District is having difficulty generating the required match in funds. It is doubtful that the school district would attempt to assume the cost of the program, some $80,000-$95,000 per year, once ARC funding terminates. Nor is it likely that providers hired by the schools for two years will continue without funding from DSS.

Should the first public school-affiliated family day care program expire, Anderson 5 officials still feel they've "demonstrated something significant—that we have the capacity—that anybody with the right resources has the capacity—of training people to provide family day care."

Satellite Family Day Care in the School District of Pickens County

Day care provided by the School District of Pickens County, a more rural and mountainous section of South Carolina than Anderson 5, dates to 1973, but developed for quite different reasons. "I guess we did it because no one else could," says Pickens Superintendent Dr. Curtis Sidden. "When ARC funds became available there was a good deal of interest in a day care program, but nobody had any personnel or facilities or way of managing it. We had a meeting with other agencies and it became clear we were the only ones who could do it. We weren't forced into it, but we didn't go out battling for it, either. Our decision was made on the basis of it being a public service." With funding from ARC, Pickens County set up three child development centers, one in a portable unit on an elementary school site, and two in former elementary school buildings. The programs serve three towns, and 158 children ages three to five.

In Pickens, family day care developed not as an extension of the child development centers or as a response to the day care needs of children under three, but as a means for enabling the School District to participate in the state kindergarten program. To qualify for state subsidy, which became available in 1969, kindergarten classes must enroll a minimum of 20 children. But in rural Pickens County—where parents earn their living by working on small farms, growing timber, and working in various scattered industrial plants—six schools were unable to meet the state requirements. Kindergarten was a new, non-mandatory program and its morning and afternoon sessions lasted only three hours, making things difficult for working parents. Transportation was hard enough to come by. So many parents found it easier to make their own arrangements for five-year-olds; children could wait until first grade, as they always had, to go to school.

If it was going to comply with state directives to reach the maximum number of five-year-olds in the district, Pickens had to find some way of providing a longer day for its kindergartners. Superintendent Curtis Sidden requested that the state Department of Education fund a full-day kindergarten. SDE couldn't do this but recommended that the district work with the Appalachian Regional Commission to develop some sort of adjunct day care program.

The solution, implemented in September 1976 with ARC funding, was family day care, officially known in Pickens County as "Satellite Day

Care to Supplement State Kindergarten Programs.'' With no income criteria attached, the program gives all families in the county the option of a full day's care for their five-year-olds. School buses take morning-session kindergartners to school, returning them at midday to a family care home where they are picked up at 4 PM by their parents (or later, by individual arrangement). For afternoon kindergartners, the procedure is reversed: parents take their children to the family day care home in the morning; the school bus brings them to school at mid-day and home at day's end. Under this double shift plan, each family day care provider can care for as many as ten children, five in the morning and five in the after-noon.

Pickens' family day care providers—there were three when the program started in September 1976—are employees of the school district, eligible for all benefits, and guaranteed a salary based on the number of children they are licensed for. A provider licensed for four children (four in the morning, four in the afternoon) earns $3,600 for the nine-month school year; a provider licensed for five earns $4,000. And providers are paid for the number on the license, not the number of children attending, so the burden is on the school district to get the children to the homes. As one school administrator says, "Five year olds are a pretty stable population; we don't get homes started unless we have some reasonable assurance that children will be there."

As in Anderson 5, the program in Pickens is managed by a family day care coordinator who hires providers and equips their homes with a variety of equipment and supplies—tables and chairs, record players and records, tape recorders, Tinker Toys, paints, paper, etc. In Pickens, however, where all the children are in school, there is a more formal link with the classroom. The coordinator visits each day care home and each classroom once or twice a week, helping the providers to continue the kindergarten curriculum. Kindergarten teachers can visit the family day care homes, and providers—who see themselves as extending the classroom—are free to call the teachers.

Since its implementation in September 1976, Pickens has opened five homes, serving some 30 children, at least half of whom, it is estimated, would not have been in kindergarten at all were it not for the program. According to Program Coordinator Jane Mahaffey, in September 1977, at the start of the program's second operational year, "We're getting calls left and right from people who say 'I can't put my child in kindergarten unless we have day care.' ''

Although plans call for the opening of 12 homes within the next year, the future of family day care in Pickens County, as in Anderson 5, is very much in doubt. ARC funding covers the period from September 1976 to June 1979; after that, if the school district wants to reach out to its five-year-olds, it will have to fund the family day care program entirely, or find some other alternative. One that is talked about is a school district or state funded full-day kindergarten. According to Jane Mahaffey, "A lot of people—a lot of parents and principals—are requesting full day kindergarten, so they wouldn't have to worry about arranging for their children. Because of the working situation. Just to know they're in one place for the day and are taken care of."

ADMINISTRATIVE STRUCTURE

Anderson 5 Family Day Care

While the family day care office is located in the Child Development Center, there is little coordination between the two programs. Anderson 5's family day care program operates largely as a unit independent of other programs in the district. However, payroll, supply and equipment purchasing, and food reimbursement procedures are all centralized through the school district.

The Family Day Care Coordinator supervises all homes and three home visitors, one professional and two paraprofessional; the coordinator is responsible to the director of the Child Development Center.

The following organizational chart locates the family day care program in relation to other district programs:

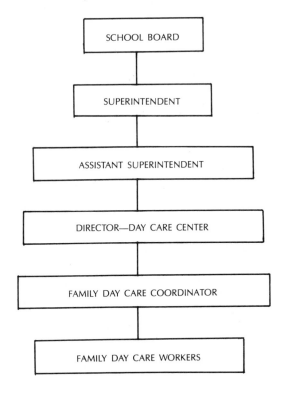

SCHOOL BOARD

SUPERINTENDENT

ASSISTANT SUPERINTENDENT

DIRECTOR—DAY CARE CENTER

FAMILY DAY CARE COORDINATOR

FAMILY DAY CARE WORKERS

Pickens County Satellite Family Day Care

As the following organizational chart indicates, Pickens Family Day Care operates as a separate unit from, but in coordination with the elementary schools.

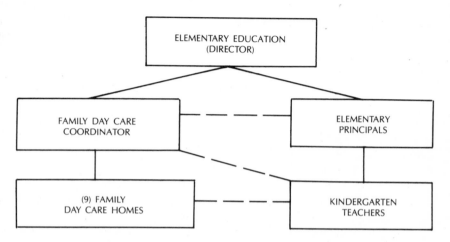

The Family Day Care Coordinator is the principal facilitator of the program. She works with the elementary principals to identify children registering for kindergarten who might need the family day care program, and to identify potential family day care providers. After hiring family day care providers, the Coordinator makes regular visits to both the day care homes and the kindergarten classroom, ensuring a coordinated curriculum.

Purchasing of all supplies and equipment is centralized through the school district.

FINANCING AND COSTS

Anderson 5 Family Day Care

Since their inception, all child development programs in Anderson 5 have been financed by a combination of ARC funds, federal funds, and in-kind contributions or certified public expenditures (CPE) from the school district. There has been no cash contribution from the district, nor is one anticipated.

The Center-Based and Home-Based programs began operating in 1972 with an initial budget of some $1 million, financed by an ARC match to Title IV-A funds. Over the next five years, Title IV-A was replaced by Title XX, and the mandatory reduction in ARC funds of 10 percent per year was replaced by school district in-kind contributions and certified public expenditures. By the end of the school year 1977, when the five year ARC funding cycle expired, the Child Development Center was financed by Title XX, with only certified public expenditures as the match. The Home-Based program was terminated as there was no available match—not even CPE—for Title XX funds.

The Family Day Care program has been financed since 1975 by Title XX funds—with ARC funds as the matching share—and by parent fees ranging from $4 to $14.95 per week. (Parent fees are determined by the following formula:

$$\frac{Weekly \ Gross \ Income}{\# \ in \ Family \ \times \ 5}$$

Even if a family has two members, the minimum listed is four; the maximum listed is ten, even if the family has more than ten members.) Current amounts of funding for the project ending in August 1977 are $50,610, ARC; $22,385, Title XX; and $6,360, parent fees. Projected costs for the third year of operation are $68,992 in ARC funds and $12,175 in parent fees.

The total cost of the Family Day Care program, which serves an average of 38 children during the entire calendar year, is approximately $80,000. The average cost per child is $2,100.

Pickens Satellite Family Day Care

The Family Day Care program in Pickens is financed largely by ARC funds, with a combination of cash and in-kind contributions as the local district match. Although there are no parent fees required for participation, those parents who use family day care beyond the program's official hours work out a "babysitting fee" with providers for the extra hours.

The breakdown of funding sources is as follows:

	ARC	School District Cash	School District In-kind (staff time of superintendent, personnel office, etc.)
1976-77	$62,450	$600	$4,300
1977-78	$77,030	$500	$7,450

The average cost per child during 1976-77, when the program served approximately 30 children, was $982. The anticipated cost per child for serving some 70 children during 1977-78 is approximately $1,000 per child at full enrollment.

ELIGIBILITY

Anderson 5 Family Day Care

Each funding source stipulates its own eligibility criteria. Approximately half the slots in the program are open on a sliding-fee scale, without regard to income, according to ARC criteria. The other half, in compliance with Department of Social Services regulations, must be divided between 60 percent current AFDC recipients and 40 percent income eligible clients.

Pickens Satellite Family Day Care

Eligibility is open to all kindergarten pupils in Pickens County. Although the program is targeted for children of working parents, there is no work requirement. During 1976-77, five out of 30 children had one parent at home while they were attending the family day care program.

PERSONNEL

Anderson 5 Family Day Care

• **Credentials.** Although they are public school employees, family day care providers are not required to have the credentials of classroom teachers. The only specific requirements are those set by the Department of Social Services: that the person be 21 years of age, not live in a trailer, pass a physical and TB test, and meet minimum space requirements per child (35 sq. ft. inside, 75 sq. ft. outside).

• **Hiring.** Screening of prospective providers is done by the Family Day Care Coordinator; if a home meets with her approval, she calls in the licensing representative from the Department of Social Services. There are no other personnel review procedures, and there is no parent input in the hiring procedure. Children are assigned to homes on the basis of available space, proximity to their home, and eligibility.

Finding providers to hire was no problem after the program established, with its first few family day care staff, that it was really going to pay people to care for children. As the coordinator says, "It's been in operation long enough to sell itself. We don't recruit; it's all by word of mouth; everybody's got friends."

• **Salary.** For a period of one year—two years beginning in September 1977—providers are employees of the school district. They receive a basic wage of $40 per week, plus $15 per week for each child in their care, and are paid weekly by the school district. Average salaries range between $85-$130 per week, or $4,420 to $6,760 for the twelve-month year, which includes eleven paid holidays and eight inservice days. Family day care staff are eligible for health insurance and life insurance; without this insurance one provider, who slipped a disk while on the job, might have been paying hospital bills for the rest of her life.

In addition, providers purchase $7 worth of groceries per child per week. They use school district purchase orders to pick up food at the local A&P. The school district provides the menu which determines which foods can be purchased. Any food costing more than the $7 per child is paid for by the provider.

Pickens Satellite Family Day Care

• **Credentials.** In accordance with policy for County Employees, family day care providers are required to have a high school diploma or equivalency. Otherwise, the same criteria apply as in Anderson 5.

• **Hiring.** Same as Anderson 5.

• **Salary.** Although they do not work under contract, family day care providers are public school employees, eligible for health care and all other benefits. During the first year of program operation, salary was pegged to the number of children taken care of. Providers with four children per session received $3,600 for the nine-month school year; those with five children per session received $4,000. In fact, however, most homes averaged three children per session or, at most, seven children for both sessions. It is expected that this will be the case during the second year of operation, and a uniform salary of $3,700 will be paid.

COORDINATION WITH ELEMENTARY SCHOOL

Anderson 5 Family Day Care

The Anderson 5 program is targeted for a population of children from six weeks to six years of age, and is coordinated with the Child Development Center program to best meet the needs of families. However, it is not coordinated with the elementary schools or with other components of the school district program.

Pickens Satellite Family Day Care

See section on Administrative Structure, page 111.

PARENT INVOLVEMENT

Anderson 5 Family Day Care

Parents can have a choice in selecting the family day care home which will care for their children, if they wish to provide transportation to a home not in direct proximity to their own.

Parent involvement is on a day-to-day basis with providers, as children are dropped off or picked up. There are no formal meetings or advisory committees for parents to be involved in policy making.

Pickens County Satellite Family Day Care

As in Anderson 5, there is no formal mechanism for parent involvement. Parental preference for a particular family day care is respected if the home is not already full. Parents can request to have their children transferred to a different home, but this has not happened.

MONITORING AND EVALUATION

In both Anderson 5 and Pickens County, the Family Day Care Coordinator is the person charged with hiring family day care providers and with evaluating their performance. Evaluation is done informally on the basis of performance, and workers who do not enjoy providing this service "weed" themselves out of the program.

In addition, both projects are given written evaluations by representatives from the State Office of Child Development.

V.

Synthesis of Findings and Recommendations

This study was not designed to be comparative in any rigorously systematic way. Each of the five communities represented was selected for its distinctiveness, a distinctiveness I have tried to capture in the individual profiles.

This section, by contrast, draws out comparisons implicit in the profiles along major programmatic dimensions. And to the extent that it can be done without violating the integrity of each individual program, this synthesis of findings and impressions attempts to address two major questions:

What are the implications of these five programs for the development of national day care policy?

In light of these five programs, what guidelines can be offered to other communities regarding utilization of the public schools as a resource for day care programs?

RECOMMENDATION AGAINST PRESUMED PRIME SPONSORSHIP

My examination of public school involvement in day care in five different communities leaves me with the impression, more strongly than ever, that there should be no presumed prime sponsorship of day care services under any national legislation. Schools, like other agencies, can play and are playing a variety of roles in the delivery of day care services. However, the nature and viability of those roles are highly dependent upon local circumstances. In some areas such as Pickens County, the rural South Carolina community included for profile here, the school system may be the only agency willing to sponsor and operate day care programs. In other areas, certain characteristics of the schools may make them unacceptable to the community as providers of day care and/or there may be other agencies with a greater interest in and capacity to provide such services.

Because the needs, resources, and histories of communities in this country are so diverse, it would be unwise to assume categorically that the schools (or any other agency) are the best possible sponsor or provider of day care; it would be equally unwise for national policy to exclude the schools as a potential provider of day care. The variety represented in this report suggests the need for an approach to national day care policy that values pluralism and local planning.

It should be pointed out here that in four of the five communities profiled, where public schools are already involved in delivering day care services, none of the people I interviewed were in favor of exclusive public school control or presumed prime sponsorship of day care. Although in favor of the arrangements they had worked out in their communities, they were wary of possible differences in need in other communities and of the need for local decision-making.

ALTERNATIVE MODELS OF PUBLIC SCHOOL INVOLVEMENT

For the most part, recent debate has emphasized the differences and incompatabilities between public schools and other possible providers of child care services; in so doing, it has largely neglected possibilities for cooperation.

My examination of five communities suggests not only that there are very different levels of public school involvement in day care, but also that cooperative models—partnerships between the schools and community or parent-controlled groups providing child care—may offer some communities especially promising directions for program development.

As detailed in their profiles and summarized in the following sections, the partnership models of Austin and Brookline combine, in different ways, major advantages of public schools (such as facilities) with some of the major advantages of private nonprofit groups: greater possibilities for parent involvement or control, more administrative flexibility, and more flexibility in staffing patterns.

FINANCING

One of the strongest arguments for a major public school role in day care has been the potential of the schools to provide a stable ongoing financial base, to relieve day care programs of the crisis-orientation to funding which drains so heavily on the energies of directors, teachers, and parents.

For the five programs profiled here, realization of such potential is neither an actuality nor a likelihood for the near future. None is supported, to any significant extent, by the general operating budget of its public school system; and none except Oakland receives any substantial support from local tax revenues (Oakland receives approximately 39% of its funding from a special tax override).

Federal Title XX dollars are the predominant source of funding in all communities except Brookline, which relies heavily (80-90%) on parent fees. Matching funds for Title XX are provided in a variety of ways, most of them somewhat precarious. South Carolina, for example, relies on funds from the Appalachian Regional Commission (ARC), which are soon due to expire; Austin uses a pilot grant from the Texas Education Authority, which has granted less money in each consecutive year; and Atlanta puts up its match in certified public expenditures (the value of buildings, administrative salaries, etc.), which can then not be used to generate other matching funds.

The most securely established programs appear to be two that are very different in nature and in sources of funding. The Oakland Children's Centers, which rely on local tax support to complement Title XX funding, are well-entrenched—albeit largely restricted to a Title XX population. Brookline's Extended Day program, by contrast, circumvents most of the fluctuations and eligibility restrictions of government funding, relying primarily on a parent-paid sliding-fee scale. It is important to note that in Brookline, the contribution of public school space and custodial services allows fees to be kept at a level much lower than would otherwise be possible.

The relative stability of the Oakland and Brookline programs does not imply that they are models easily transferable to other communities. Local tax support of the Oakland programs was initiated some twenty years ago; given the financial constraints of so many school systems, it is unlikely to be initiated in many other communities today. In Brookline, a relatively high level of income means that a sliding-fee scale can generate enough money to support a program; in poorer communities, reliance on sliding fee scales, even with the contribution of public school space and custodial services, might not provide enough of the money necessary to hire teachers, purchase supplies, and so forth.

If the patterns of funding in these five communities are at all indicative of conditions elsewhere, day care affiliated with the schools *or any other organizations* will not achieve more financial stability unless significant actions are taken at both the federal and state levels. An infusion of federal funds is needed *along with* aggressive state implementation of Title XX sliding-fee scales, the only existing means of broadening both eligibility and parent payments for day care.

In the absence of new federal funding, the models presented here with the greatest financial viability in other communities are the partnerships, Brookline and Austin. Because they use public school facilities without public school salary scales, each can maximize the utilization for services of its available funding (Title XX in Austin, parent fees in Brookline).

ELIGIBILITY

When it comes to eligibility, the overall picture presented by these five public school-affiliated programs is the same as it is for most day care programs in the country, regardless of their auspices: segregation by income.

Almost all programs have income criteria for eligibility, determined by their sources of funding. Three of the five programs—Atlanta, Austin, and Oakland—are largely restricted to Title XX eligible families (2% of families using the Oakland Children's Centers are not eligible for Title XX, and pay on a sliding-fee scale). Eligibility is somewhat broader in South Carolina's family day care programs, because one is fully and the other partially funded by the Appalachian Regional Commission. Eligibility is broadest in Brookline's program, which is the least dependent on federal or state funding. The program is open to all children who attend the schools, regardless of income; some 10% are paid for by Title XX, the rest by parent fees on a sliding scale.

Unless federal funding guidelines change substantially and unless states begin aggressively implementing sliding-fee scales, this pattern of Title XX versus non-Title XX programs is likely to continue, no matter what agencies are sponsoring or operating day care programs.

PERSONNEL

Because staff requirements, hiring procedures, and salary levels so largely determine the composition and the costs of any day care program, the implications of public school involvement for personnel practices has been a sensitive, and central, issue in the current debate.

The five programs profiled here suggest that:

(1) The extent to which the personnel practices of school-affiliated programs integrate day care staff with other school personnel varies considerably from community to community.

In the Brookline Extended Day program, for example, which is officially part of the schools, teachers are not school employees, though they are hired, in part, by the school principal. In South Carolina, family day care providers *are* school employees—and, therefore, eligible for certain insurance benefits—but they do not have to meet public school teaching requirements. In Atlanta, day care teachers receive a salary equal to their public school colleagues, but they work the full year; in Oakland, credentialed teachers receive the regular school salary and work the regular 180-day school year.

(2) The application of public school requirements to day care staff naturally increases costs and, in so doing, builds in a greater tension, if not conflict, between the ability of the system to meet the needs of its personnel and the needs of children and families for day care.

In Atlanta, for example, where new monies for day care are not available, a six-year emphasis on hiring teachers with graduate degrees has led to a choice between cutting back services and cutting back on the credentials required of day care teachers. It is a somewhat bitter pill for the schools to have to retrench educational standards for staff, but it is the only way to continue providing services.

In Oakland, the recent achievement of parity meets the needs of day care teachers for equitable salary, and the needs of the school system to be able to transfer personnel from elementary school to day care assignments; but the 180-day work year also means that more and more children will face discontinuity in their caregivers. This dilemma seems likely to increase in Oakland and to present itself to other communities where parity is achieved. The obvious solution for meeting the needs of both children and teachers would be to reduce the vacation time of day care teachers while compensating them in salary for a longer work year. However, such a solution would be costly (regular teachers are more expensive than substitute teachers), and would lead—in the absence of increased funding—to yet another conflict between teacher needs and service needs.

If either Atlanta or Oakland is indicative, communities which try to apply existing school personnel practices to the operation of day care will experience significant strains and will be forced either to cut back in services or to reduce—as Atlanta is now doing—their educational requirements for day care teachers. According to *preliminary* findings of the National Day Care Study, conducted by Abt Associates for the Administration for Children, Youth, and Families, such modification might not result in any loss in the quality of care that children receive. Contrary to the initial premises of the Atlanta program and others which have developed on the traditional public school model, the Abt study suggests that "formal education" has less to do with caregiver quality than does "specialization in a child-related field," which might be acquired in a variety of settings, including college or high school courses, vocational training and on-the-job training programs.

(3) Partnership arrangements between public schools and private nonprofit agencies allow for more flexible personnel policies, thereby reducing conflicts between service needs and teacher needs.

Both Austin and Brookline seem to have found a middle ground that may be instructive for other communities. Although both programs are part of their respective school systems, teachers are employees of private nonprofit corporations and are paid on a separate scale. In Austin, where teachers are employed by Child, Inc. but required to meet the minimum educational requirements of the School District, they are paid somewhat above the usual Child, Inc. scale, and somewhat below the regular public school scale. In Brookline, where there are no specific educational requirements, each parent-controlled board sets its own salary level. Because neither program has been grafted onto an existing public school salary schedule, each has more flexibility in the difficult attempt to balance the need of day care teachers for a decent salary and the need of families for services.

COORDINATION WITH ELEMENTARY SCHOOLS

The extent to which—and the ways in which—day care should or might be coordinated with various aspects of elementary school programs has been a recurring issue in the debate. Proponents of school-sponsored or -operated day care often point to the possibility of a more continuous educational experience for the child; opponents fear that schools will inappropriately shape day care classrooms in an academic mold.

Three of the programs profiled here—Oakland, Atlanta, and Brookline—are located in or adjacent to elementary schools. In Oakland and Atlanta, the two which are most highly integrated within the public school administrative structure, some attempts are being made to build links between day care and the elementary grades, for the explicit purpose of reinforcing the elementary curriculum. While such attempts might well be increased in the future, they appear at present to be haphazard, at best. (In Brookline, there are no such explicit attempts at coordination.)

In all of these school-based programs, including Brookline, other aspects of coordination seem to be more salient than curriculum. For one, day care teachers often feel that elementary school teachers are misinformed about day care, that they share the popular public stigma, and that no real coordination will ever take place unless day care is regarded with higher status. Moreover, the establishment of guidelines for sharing is a very important issue for those programs—such as Brookline and Atlanta—where day care for school age children has had to double up with regular classroom space.

For all aspects of coordination, the school principal emerges as a key figure. In those programs where the principal understands and is clearly supportive of day care, there appears to be more coordination between elementary and day care staff, and guidelines for shared space are worked out. Often, however, principals have little understanding of what day care is, or resent being assigned yet another responsibility.

Communities choosing to use public schools in any way as a resource for day care would best facilitate coordination by informing, educating, and enlisting the support of their school principals.

PARENT INVOLVEMENT

While all participants in the current debate are in favor of parental involvement, there is considerable disagreement about *how* and *how much* parents should or could be involved in decision-making if day care is to be affiliated with the schools. The programs profiled here represent several levels of involvement and may be instructive in pointing towards national guidelines.

The three programs that are most closely integrated with the school system have the lowest levels of *formally structured* parental input in decision-making. Neither of South Carolina's family day care programs, for example, has a formal mechanism for parent involvement (though parents do choose their family day care homes). Atlanta and Oakland have district level Parent Advisory Committees, neither of which has responsibility for hiring or budget setting. However, there appears to be *considerable* variation from center to center in parent involvement, often depending on the center director or mix of parents. In some instances in Oakland, this includes a *de facto* parental hiring of staff, though this is not a feature of the overall system.

The two partnership models—Brookline and Austin—are *structured* to allow for the greatest amount of parent involvement, though there are major differences between them in actual level of that involvement. In Brookline, which has the highest level of parent involvement, each of the programs—though officially part of the school system—is designed and administered by a separate parent group as a nonprofit corporation. Parents in these programs hire staff, set budgets, and set general directions or "curriculum." The Austin program, insofar as it operates under Child, Inc., has a board of directors heavily composed of parents; while none of these are currently the teen-aged parents who use the program that Child, Inc. runs in conjunction with the Austin Independent School District, the potential for such involvement clearly exists. In all cases, it should be noted, regardless of structure, actual levels of parent involvement appear highly dependent on the personalities involved, especially those of day care directors and parents in leadership positions.

Taken together, these five programs do suggest some directions for national policy. Given our inability to legislate warm and accepting environments, these programs suggest that parental involvement will not be guaranteed, no matter what the auspices of the program, without specific prescription of parental responsibility for major programmatic decisions, as in Brookline. However, the level of parental control that exists in Brookline might not be practically achievable or desirable in other communities. And to prescribe parent control nationally via legislation or regulations might well be counterproductive, ignoring both the preferences and the constraints of many working parents and unintentionally subverting some of the informal but meaningful opportunities for involvement that can occur without it. A more realistic and responsive course might be to guarantee by legislation *and regulatory language*—the right of parental involvement in specific areas of decision-making, without requiring that parents assume control. Such a policy might safeguard opportunities for real parental involvement, while allowing each community to work out its own specific plans.

VI.

What Lies Ahead?

If the programs profiled in this report are any indication, it is unlikely that the public education system in these communities, or in many others throughout the country, will start picking up the cost of day care as part of the regular school budget during the next few years. Like all forms of publicly supported day care in this country, the future of school-related care will depend on prospects for any new federal legislation.

Opinions regarding the prospects for such legislation differ considerably. To many, the Vice Presidency of Walter Mondale, co-architect of the last two major day care bills and a persistent champion of services for children and families, augurs well. As Marilyn Rauth, one of the coordinators of the AFT "campaign" says, "I'm sure day care isn't Carter's top priority. But with Mondale close to the top the prospects are brighter than ever. I don't think we'll have a bill vetoed."

However, others seriously question whether another major day care bill will ever make it to the President's desk. The effects of an anonymous right-wing smear campaign against the Child and Family Services Act of 1975—which produced more letters to Congress than any recent issue including Vietnam—were devastating and may explain Congressional reluctance to come forth with another legislative initiative. In the most recent session, for example, only one comprehensive child care bill has been introduced, S.2505, by Congressman Roybal, a California Democrat. According to one Senate staffer, "Most members of Congress won't go near any day care bill now because they're afraid of it. Members of Congress are very sensitive to their constituency. They didn't get any letters from the pro people. They just got letters from crazies saying day care will destroy the family. Even if you know the basis of that information is incorrect, it's going to scare you off from getting involved."

According to another former Congressional staffer who played a significant role in passage of 1971 child care legislation, "There's a lot of stuff coming out saying there's no need for a national day care program, that the supply of day care is sufficient to meet the demand. So the ball is back in our court in terms of proving there's a need.''

Assertion of that need may be just around the corner. Senator Alan Cranston (D-California), who took over the chair of the Senate Subcommittee on Child and Human Development from Senator Mondale, opened another round of child care hearings in November 1977, and is planning to introduce new legislation in the summer or fall of 1978. However, most child care advocates agree that any major legislative initiative will have at least to involve the cooperation of the Carter administration.

Whether or not the administration will cooperate, even with Walter Mondale as Vice President, is unclear, as is its position on child care. Since comprehensive welfare reform is the administration's top domestic priority, the politics of child care seem inextricably tied, as they always have been, to the politics of welfare.[1] However, in April 1978, President Carter endorsed a bill (S.991) introduced by Connecticut Senator Abraham Ribicoff, former Secretary of HEW, to establish a separate cabinet level Department of Education. Authority for Head Start, the nation's most politically attractive child development program, would be transferred to the proposed department, paving the way, some have argued, for the transfer to Education of other child care programs that already exist or that might be generated by new legislation.

What all this adds up to is a state of suspended animation in federal day care policy. While the White House professes concern with broadranging policies that will ''strengthen the American family,'' and tries to steer its welfare reform package through Congress, groups concerned about day care prime sponsorship have been playing a holding action, waiting for the Congress or the administration to make its move.

The AFT, for example, which Gil Steiner sees as the only potentially significant lobby for day care, isn't exactly charging ahead with its Action Program for ''Putting Early Childhood and Day Care Services Into the Public Schools,'' which was designed, at the time of the Child and Family Services Act, ''to create a groundswell of local interest . . . that will be felt by both the Congress and the President.''[2] In 1977 the union did produce an attractive anthology-text, *Early Childhood,* for use in college courses, which includes articles by Albert Shanker and other AFT representatives explaining why a comprehensive child care policy is only feasible with public school prime sponsorship.[3] But according to Marilyn Rauth, ''Because of the lack of national legislation, there are no great progress reports to be made. We're still monitoring the situation at the national level and we do workshops whenever we're asked. We've got the campaign on a low burner. We can activate it at any time. The important thing is that the network is in place. But the timing isn't right.''

Advocacy groups opposed to public school prime sponsorship are also concerned with proper timing. In spring 1977, a loose-knit group of some 85 organizations, called the Ad Hoc Child Development Coalition, led by Children's Defense Fund director Marian Wright Edelman, sent a letter to President Carter pledging their "commitment to work with [the administration] to shape a program that provides quality services and that can win broad support." Almost simultaneously, child care advocates helped persuade Senator Charles Mathias of Maryland to refrain from introducing a bill calling for early education in the public schools (half-day programs for three- and four-year-olds). According to Mathias's aide, Kent Steincamp, "The Senator hasn't introduced it and he probably won't because the natural supporters, the constituency, felt it would defeat their attempts to get broader and higher priority legislation passed, legislation for child care as opposed to early education."

By December 1977, when the only response the Ad Hoc Child Development Coalition had from the administration was a three-paragraph letter assuring them that HEW Secretary Joseph Califano would work with them "in creating a comprehensive family policy," the Coalition agreed to begin drafting their own legislation, taking as a first step a review of the strengths and weaknesses of the 1975 Child and Family Services bill.[4] (The Coalition hope to work closely with Senator Cranston.)

In the absence of any major new federal day care legislation, the most significant activities regarding the "public school question" will continue to occur at the local level. Faced with declining enrollments, it seems inevitable that more and more school systems will become concerned about their "responsibility" to young children. Increasing numbers of working parents will become concerned about the care of their children after school and about the ways the school or other agencies might assist them. Perhaps most significant of all will be the implications of recent landmark federal legislation for the handicapped (PL 94-142) which requires that all school districts make programs available for handicapped children, aged 3 and up, by September 1978. But if school districts are not to segregate special needs children, then PL 94-142 may hasten the entry of the public schools towards the provision of services—at least on a half-day basis, to all three-year-olds.

This is not to suggest the imminence of any major effort by school districts around the country to become involved in day care. Given the financial plight of most school systems, it is unlikely that many would become involved at local taxpayer expense. And even if federal dollars were available, many would be flatly opposed to day care on the grounds that it is not an appropriate school function or that the schools have already been asked to do too much.

It is to suggest, however, that in the absence of federal dollars or of legislation specifying the schools or some other agency as a prime sponsor, communities will have little choice but to figure out, in their own terms, the role (if any) of schools and other agencies in day care delivery. Whether or not this will give rise to more cooperative arrangements between schools and parent groups (as in Brookline) or between schools and private agencies (as in Austin), it is unlikely that many communities will be able to afford considering the role of the public schools in day care as an either-or proposition.

The arrangements worked out will no doubt vary from community to community, based on the capability, power, and influence of schools, other agencies, and parents. That is, in the short term, the matter of prime sponsorship will be played out at the local level, and in terms of community politics, not national politics.

It may well be that at the local level there is a better chance to avoid what Kamerman and Kahn have identified as one of the major problems with national day care planning in this country: i.e., the persistent effort—reflected so clearly in the "prime sponsorship" debate—to "categorize," to define programs as day care or as education according to their institutional auspices, rather than according to the functions they perform for both children and parents. As Kamerman and Kahn say, "The variability within each program category (day care, preschool) is as great as the variation between them. Thus, school-based programs may be developmental, in the day care sense, and day care programs may make a significant educational contribution."[5]

In order to avoid categorical definitions, national child care policy may have to do what local communities are now being forced to do. That is, at the local level, as Kamerman and Kahn suggest, "Planning should . . . look at total resource and the potentials in each program category in relation to the diversity of needs."[6]

A national system that respects such diversity—among parents, children, and communities—is likely to be the most responsive system. "All this speaks for pluralism, choice, alternatives—and for a diversity of child care administrative and programming patterns as well. Not easy for policy makers—but probably better for children."[7]

VI.

Notes

I. Introduction: About this Report

[1] As of this writing, I know of only two publications that look more particularly at school involvement, both of them excellent: W. Norton Grubb and Marvin Lazerson, "Child Care, Government Financing, and the Public Schools: Lessons from the California Children's Centers," *School Review* (Vol. 86, No. 1, November 1977), pp. 5-37; and Carol E. Joffe, *Friendly Intruders: Childcare Professionals and Family Life* (Berkeley: University of California Press, 1977). Joffe's book is based on a study of half-day early education programs in the Berkeley Unified School District.

[2] For a similar "finding" about day care leadership, discussed at much greater length and in detail, see Ellen Galinsky and William H. Hooks, *The New Extended Family: Day Care that Works* (Boston: Houghton Mifflin, 1977), pp. 239-253. Also see Richard Ruopp et al., *Day Care Guide for Administrators, Teachers, and Parents* (Cambridge: MIT Press, 1973).

[3] W. Norton Grubb, "Alternative Futures for Child Care," Childhood and Government Project Working Paper #11 (Berkeley: Childhood and Government Project, Earl Warren Legal Institute, School of Law, University of California, 1977).

[4] At this writing, I am a consultant on Project Connections, a national research and demonstration effort jointly funded by the Ford Foundation and the Administration for Children, Youth, and Families, which is examining child care information and referral services. The project is being conducted by American Institutes for Research, 22 Hilliard Street, Cambridge, MA 02138.

[5] According to the best available estimate of day care "supply" — the National Day Care Center Study conducted by Abt Associates — there are between 700 and 800 full-day Head Starts located either in or out of schools, with over 100 of them in Mississippi; see Craig Coelen, *National Supply of Center Day Care*, 1975-1976, Abt Associates, Inc.: Cambridge, MA, scheduled for publication, fall 1978. Data from the federal agency responsible for Head Start—the ACYF in HEW—is broken down by auspices but combines figures for full-day, full-year programs with those for part-day, full-year programs. According to an ACYF memo of May 3, 1978, there were in FY 76 1,122 Head Start grantees, of which 103 were school systems; schools were receiving $15,000,000 out of a total $391,000,000 to provide services for some 14,307 children out of a total 281,000.

II. The Emergence of the "Public School Question"

[1] Barbara Bowman, "Should the Public Schools Control Child Care Services?" in *Early Childhood Education; It's an Art? It's a Science?*, ed., J. D. Andrews (Washington, D.C.: National Association for the Education of Young Children, 1976), p. 111.

[2] Albert Shanker, "Early Childhood Education is a Job for the Public Schools," in "Where We Stand: A Weekly Column of Comment on Public Education," *New York Times*, Sunday September 8, 1974, Section E, p. 11.

[3]The thrust of Dr. Martin's argument is available in "Who Will Deliver Education to Pre-school Children?" in *One Child Indivisible*, ed. J. D. Andrews (Washington, D.C.: National Association for the Education of Young Children, 1975), pp. 97-133; also in an unpublished speech, "Public Policy and Early Childhood Education," presented to the AFT in Honolulu on July 12, 1975. Dr. Martin makes it clear, however, in a personal interview, that he has never been lobbying for or with the AFT: "I have been looking at early education strictly from the point of view of service to people—if you want to maximize the service, what do you do?"

[4]Interagency Task Force on Youth Care and Rehabilitation, *A Plan for Child and Youth Care in Texas* (Austin: Office of the Governor, 1974), p. 35.

[5]In June 1977, the NFIE document was in final draft form for presentation to the NEA membership. The NFIE document went to the executive committee of NEA in late fall 1977 but is still under study. According to Mr. John Sullivan, NEA Director of Instruction and Professional Development, "The basic reason they haven't done anything about it is be-cause developing an active policy would take an investment of resources that aren't avail-able now."

[6]Gilbert Y. Steiner, *The Children's Cause* (Washington, D.C.: The Brookings Institution, 1976), pp. 116-117, 244, 243, 247. Citations in the text follow the page sequence as listed here.

[7]Eugenia Kemble, "Should the Public Schools Control Child Care Services?" in *Early Childhood Education: It's an Art? It's a Science?*, ed., J. D. Andrews (Washington, D.C., 1976), p. 126.

[8]Susan Hunsinger and Shelley Kessler, "Child Care Policy: Maximizing Family Choice," Staff Working Paper for the Carnegie Council on Children, submitted as Testimony on the Child and Family Services Act, 1975, Joint Hearings before the Senate Subcommittee on Children and Youth, Senate Subcommittee on Employment, Poverty, and Migratory Labor, and House Subcommittee on Select Education, 94th Congress, 1st session, part 9, p. 2262.

[9]W. Norton Grubb, "Alternative Futures for Child Care," Childhood and Government Working Paper #11 (Berkeley: Childhood and Government Project, School of Law, Univer-sity of California), p. 24. The citation from Grubb should not be misconstrued to indicate that he supports public school prime sponsorship; he is, in fact, vehemently opposed to such a plan.

[10]David Sheehan, *The Children's Puzzle: A Study of Services to Children in Massachu-setts* (Boston: University of Massachusetts Institute for Governmental Services, 1977), p. A-3.

[11]Data on Head Start provided by Administration for Children, Youth, and Families, HEW, memo of May 3, 1978.

[12]National Center for Education Statistics, Division of Education, Department of Health, Education, and Welfare, *Statistics of Public Elementary and Secondary Day Schools, Fall 1977*. Scheduled for publication, fall 1978.

[13]Dr. Wood's recommendations were reported in the *Boston Globe*, April 25, 1977, and confirmed in a letter to me of May 5, 1977 as being one of many recommendations he made about the "general problems of education" in America.

[14]Information about Minnesota's Early Childhood and Family Education Programs is available from the Minnesota Council on Quality Education, % State Department of Educa-tion, 718 Capitol Square Bldg., St. Paul, Minnesota 55101.

[15]Craig Coelen, *National Supply of Center Day Care, 1975-1976*, Abt Associates, Inc.: Cambridge, MA, scheduled for publication, fall 1978.

[16]W. Norton Grubb, "Alternative Futures for Child Care," p. 18, p. 1.

III. Major Issues in the Debate

[1]Gwen Morgan, "The Trouble with Title XX," (Washington, D.C.: Day Care and Child Development Council of America, 1977), p. 17.

[2]AFT Task Force on Educational Issues, *Putting Early Childhood and Day Care Services into the Public Schools: The Position of the American Federation of Teachers and An Action Plan for Promoting It* (Washington, D.C.: AFT, 1976), p. 7. From here on, reference to this publication will be abbreviated as AFT Task Force.

[3] AFT Task Force, p. 16.

[4] Marvin Lazerson, "The Historical Antecedents of Early Childhood Education," in *Early Childhood Education: The Seventy-First Yearbook of the National Society for the Study of Education,* Part II (Chicago: University of Chicago Press, 1972).

[5] Edwin W. Martin, "Public Policy and Early Childhood Education: A Buddhist Garden" in *Early Childhood,* ed. Barry Persky and Leonard Golubchick in cooperation with the American Federation of Teachers (Wayne, NJ: Avery Publishing Group, Inc., 1977), p. 17.

[6] AFT Task Force, p. 11, p. 48.

[7] Barbara Bowman, "Should the Public Schools Control Child Care Services?" in *Early Childhood Education: It's an Art? It's a Science?,* ed. J. D. Andrews (Washington, D.C.: National Association for the Education of Young Children, 1976), pp. 114-115.

[8] Marian Wright Edelman, Testimony on Child and Family Services Act, 1975, Joint Hearings, part 1, p. 144.

[9] William B. Welsh, Executive Director for Legislative and Political Affairs of the American Federation of State, County and Municipal Employees, Testimony on the Child and Family Services Act, 1975, Joint Hearings, part 9, p. 1971.

[10] AFT Task Force, p. 48.

[11] AFT Task Force, p. 48.

[12] Barbara Bowman, p. 115.

[13] W. Norton Grubb and Marvin Lazerson, "Public School Control of Child Care: Lessons from the California Children's Centers" (Berkeley: Childhood and Government Project, School of Law, University of California, 1975), unpublished manuscript, p. 77. Grubb and Lazerson make the same point in different words in their *School Review* article, p. 23.

[14] Ted Taylor, "Who Will Deliver Education to Preschool Children?" in *One Child Indivisible,* ed., J. D. Andrews (Washington, D.C.: National Association for the Education of Young Children, 1976), p. 124.

[15] Barbara Bowman, p. 115.

[16] William B. Welsh, AFSCME, Testimony on Child and Family Services Act, 1975, part 9, p. 1971.

[17] Susan Hunsinger and Shelly Kessler, "Child Care Policy: Maximizing Family Choice," Testimony on Child and Family Services Act, 1975, Joint Hearings, part 9, p. 2252.

[18] AFT Task Force, p. 54.

[19] AFT Task Force, p. 13.

[20] William B. Welsh, AFSCME, Testimony, part 9, p. 1972.

[21] Congressional Budget Office, "Elementary, Secondary, and Vocational Education: An Examination of Alternative Federal Roles," (Washington, D.C.: Congressional Budget Office, 1977), p. 45.

[22] Mary Potter Rowe and Ralph D. Husby, "Economics of Child Care: Costs, Needs, and Issues," in *Child Care–Who Cares?* ed., Pamela Roby (New York: Basic Books, 1973), p. 117.

[23] AFT Task Force, p. 23.

[24] Edwin Martin, "Who Will Deliver Education to Preschool Children?" in *One Child Indivisible,* ed., J. D. Andrews (Washington, D.C.: NAEYC), p. 114.

[25] Ted Taylor, "Who Will Deliver Education to Preschool Children?" p. 125.

[26] Greater Minneapolis Day Care Association, "Position Paper on Day Care and the Public Schools," p. 4.

[27] AFT Task Force, p. 15.

[28] AFT Task Force, p. 71.

[29] James Harris, Testimony on Child and Family Services Act, 1975, Joint Hearings, part 7, p. 1234.

[30] Edwin Martin, "Who Will Deliver Education to Preschool Children?" p. 115.

[31] Marian Wright Edelman, Testimony on the Child and Family Services Act of 1975, Joint Hearings, part 1, p. 140.

[32] Barbara Bowman, p. 114.

[33] Greater Minneapolis Day Care Association, "Position Paper on Day Care and the Public Schools," p. 4.

[34] Ted Taylor, "Who Will Deliver Education to Preschool Children?" p. 125.

[35] AFT Task Force, p. 71

132   DAY CARE AND THE PUBLIC SCHOOLS

132   DAY CARE AND THE PUBLIC SCHOOLS

36Joyce Black and Marjorie Grossett, "To the Editor," *New York Times,* August 14, 1975.

37Barbara Bowman, p. 114.

38Richard Ruopp, Jeffrey Travers, et al., *National Day Care Study Preliminary Findings and Their Implications,* 31 January 1978, (Cambridge, MA:Abt Associates, Inc., 1978).

39Marian Wright Edelman, Testimony on Child and Family Services Act, 1975, Joint Hearings, part 1, p. 142.

40AFT Task Force, p. 94.

41AFT Task Force, p. 14.

42Jerome M. Hughes, "The Home as an Academy for Learning," in *The National Elementary Principal,* vol. 55, n. 6 (July/August 1976), p. 28.

43William B. Welsh, AFSCME, Testimony on Child and Family Services Act, 1975, Joint Hearings, part 9, p. 1972.

44Greater Minneapolis Day Care Association, "Position Paper on Public Schools," p. 4.

45Susan Hunsinger and Shelley Kessler, "Child Care Policy: Maximizing Family Choice," Staff Working Paper Prepared for the Carnegie Council on Children, Submitted as Testimony on Child and Family Services Act, 1975, Joint Hearings, part 9, p. 2251.

46W. Norton Grubb and Marvin Lazerson, "Child Care, Government Financing, and the Public Schools: Lessons from the California Children's Centers," *School Review,* vol. 86, no. 1 (November 1977), p. 26.

47Ibid., p. 29.

IV. Profiles (Footnotes in text)

V. Synthesis and Recommendations

1Richard Ruopp, Jeffrey Travers, et al. *National Day Care Study Preliminary Findings and Their Implications, 31 January 1978,* (Cambridge, MA: Abt Associates, Inc.), p. 2.

VI. What Lies Ahead?

1In December 1977, the House welfare reform subcommittee accepted as part of the Comprehensive Welfare Reform Bill (HR 9030) an amendment proposed by Representative Andrew Jacobs, Jr. (D-Indiana) to establish a three-year $126,000 pilot project to use empty public school classrooms as a base for half-day Head Start-type programs. As a Jacobs' aide suggested, however, "This is at very preliminary stages, subject to changes during another round with the subcommittee, the full committee, and the House floor, not to mention the Senate and the administration!"

2AFT Task Force, p. 15. Steiner's view is outlined in *The Children's Cause* (Washington, D.C.: The Brookings Institutions, 1976).

3Barry Persky and Leonard Golubchick, eds. in cooperation with the American Federation of Teachers, *Early Childhood* (Wayne, NJ: Avery Publishing Group, Inc., 1977).

4Marian Wright Edelman, Memorandum to Parties Interested in Ad Hoc Child Development Coalition (December 13, 1977); the memorandum, along with a copy of a letter from Stuart E. Eizenstat, Assistant to the President for Domestic Affairs and Policy, is available from the Children's Defense Fund, Washington Research Project, Inc., 1520 New Hampshire Avenue, N.W., Washington, D.C. 20036.

5Sheila B. Kamerman and Alfred J. Kahn, *Social Services in the United States: Policies and Programs* (Philadelphia: Temple University Press, 1976), p. 130.

6Ibid., p. 130.

7Ibid., p. 135.

VIII.

Annotated Bibliography

Many books and articles address, either tangentially or implicitly, the "public school question." Following is a list of selected publications with the most direct bearing on the issue.

AFT Task Force on Educational Issues. *Putting Early Childhood and Day Care Services into the Public Schools: The Position of the American Federation of Teachers and An Action Plan for Promoting It.* Washington, D.C.: AFT, 1976.

    Complete exposition of the AFT's arguments for presumed prime sponsorship. Highly readable orientation to the pro-public school side of the debate.

Bergstrom, Joan M. and Morgan, Gwen. *Issues in the Design of a Delivery System for Day Care and Child Development Services to Children and Their Families.* Washington, D.C.: Day Care and Child Development Council of America, Inc., 1975.

    Provocative argument for the development of a day care delivery system with a "preventive" rather than a "pathological" orientation. Recommends local sponsorship not by the public schools but by local Councils for Children and Families, and provides guidelines for the establishment of such Councils.

Bowman, Barbara and Kemble, Eugenia. "Should the Public Schools Control Child Care Services?" In *Early Childhood Education: It's an Art? It's a Science?,* edited by J. D. Andrews. Washington, D.C.: National Association for the Education of Young Children, 1976.

    Transcript of a debate at the 1975 annual NAEYC conference. Bowman, formerly Director of the Erikson Institute in Chicago, says no; Kemble, who chairs the AFT Task Force on Education Issues, says yes.

Congressional Budget Office. *Elementary, Secondary, and Vocational Education: An Examination of Alternative Federal Roles.* Washington, D.C.: Congressional Budget Office, 1977.

    Included in this highly readable analysis of possible federal strategies, their costs and effects, is a discussion of federal financial support for a universal preschool program.

Edelman, Marian Wright. *Memorandum to Parties Interested in Ad Hoc Child Development Coalition* (December 13, 1977).

The memorandum, along with a copy of a letter from Stuart E. Eizenstat, Assistant to the President for Domestic Affairs and Policy, is available from the Children's Defense Fund, Washington Research Project, Inc., 1520 New Hampshire Avenue, N.W., Washington, D.C. 20036.

Fishhaut, Erna H. and Pastor, Donald. "Should the Public Schools Be Entrusted with Preschool Education: A Critique of the AFT Proposals." *School Review* 86 (November, 1977): 38-49.

Fishhaut, who was for 10 years a day-care licensing consultant for the state of Minnesota, here provides one of the most recent rejoinders to the AFT position.

Galinsky, Ellen and Hooks, William H. *The New Extended Family: Day Care that Works.* Boston: Houghton Mifflin, 1977.

Highly readable and sensitive profiles of a wide variety of day care programs, including a public school program for teen-age mothers and their children in Philadelphia, Pennsylvania. Special attention to the people and the leaders so crucial to the success of any type of child care program.

Greenman, James. "Day Care in the Schools? A Response to the Position of the AFT." *Young Children* 33 (May, 1978): 4-15.

This most recent of rejoinders to the AFT argument brings some new language into the debate: the difference between "idiographic" and "nomothetic" orientations.

Grubb, Norton, W. "Alternative Futures for Child Care," Childhood and Government Project Working Paper #11. Berkeley: Childhood and Government Project, Earl Warren Legal Institute, School of Law, University of California, 1977.

Provocative and clearly written analysis of two radically different types of child care delivery systems: a national day care program based in the public schools and a highly diverse program that puts a premium on parent choice and provides the supports necessary to make such choices. Grubb argues in favor of the latter.

Grubb, Norton W. and Lazerson, Marvin. "Child Care, Government Financing, and the Public Schools: Lessons from the California Children's Centers." *School Review* 86 (November, 1977): 5-37.

Traces the history of the most extensive day care program in the country operating under the auspices of the public education system, and provides a thoughtful analysis of the implications of that history for current child care policy. A carefully researched and reasoned argument against public school prime sponsorship, with excellent notes and bibliography.

Hughes, Jerome M. "The Home as an Academy for Learning." *The National Elementary Principal* (July/August 1976).

Minnesota State Senator Hughes argues the need for a combination of pre-school and parent education based in the public schools. Hughes is largely responsible for his state's pilot effort in this area, the Child and Family Education Program.

Joffe, Carol E. *Friendly Intruders: Childcare Professionals and Family Life.* Berkeley: University of California Press, 1977.

A carefully wrought case study of early education programs delivered through the Berkeley public schools. Joffe pays particular attention to the professionalization of child care services as delivered through the schools, to differences in the expectations of black and white parents, and to the relationship between child care and family life.

Kamerman, Sheila B. and Kahn, Alfred J. *Social Services in the United States: Policies and Programs.* Philadelphia: Temple University Press, 1976.

This overview of the nation's social services provides the most comprehensive and orderly of available tours through the complex world of government day care programs and policies.

Levitan, Sar and Alderman, Karen. *Child Car and ABC's Too.* Baltimore: Johns Hopkins Press, 1975.

Overview of government programs and policies in the areas of day care and early education which forecasts the expansion of public responsibility for preschool but not day care.

Martin, Edwin W. "Public Policy and Early Childhood Education: A Buddhist Garden." In *Early Childhood,* edited by Barry Persky and Leonard Golubchick, in cooperation with the American Federation of Teachers. Wayne, N.J.: Avery Publishing Group, Inc., 1977.

A now classic statement by the Acting Deputy Commissioner for Education of the Handicapped about the need for a uniform delivery system based in the public schools.

Morgan, Gwen. *The Trouble with Title XX.* Washington, D.C.: Day Care and Child Development Council of America, 1977.

A lucid analysis of Title XX as it pertains to day care; along the way, Morgan argues against presumed public school prime sponsorship.

Persky, Barry and Golubchick, Leonard, eds., in cooperation with the American Federation of Teachers. *Early Childhood.* Wayne, N.J.: Avery Publishing Group, Inc., 1977.

Anthology covering a wide range of topics in early childhood education and day care: history, theory, curriculum, training, etc. Among the first selections are Albert Shanker's Congressional testimony regarding public school prime sponsorship and Edwin Martin's "Buddhist garden" speech, which suggests that schools provide a logical delivery system for day care.

Prescott, Elizabeth; Millich, Cynthia; and Jones, Elizabeth. *The Politics of Day Care.* Washington, D.C.: National Association for the Education of Young Children, 1972.

Carefully done case studies of several different types of California day care programs, including a Children's Centers program. The work of this Pacific Oaks group is always especially sensitive to the environments in which children live.

Rowe, Mary Potter and Husby, Ralph D. "Economics of Child Care: Costs, Needs, and Issues." In *Child Care—Who Cares?* edited by Pamela Roby. New York: Basic Books, 1973.

Lucid and succinct examination of the complexities of determining the costs of day care; projected cost-estimates for different types of delivery systems, along with their implications for national policy.

Ruopp, Richard et al. *Day Care Guide for Administrators, Teachers, and Parents.* Cambridge: MIT Press, 1973.

Although it does not address the public school question, this book is one of the few that spells out the importance of leadership to the success of any type of day care program.

Ruopp, Richard, Travers, Jeffrey, et al. *National Day Care Study Preliminary Findings and Their Implications, 31 January 1978.* Cambridge, Massachusetts: Abt Associates, Inc., 1978.

Findings from this major policy study will have ramifications for many aspects of day care policy in the years ahead. Preliminary findings have particular bearing on arguments about personnel and credentialing.

Shanker, Albert. "Early Childhood Education is a Job for the Public Schools" in "Where We Stand: A Weekly Column of Comment on Public Education," *New York Times.* Sunday, September 8, 1974: Section E, p. 11.

One of the AFT President's earliest pronouncements on the topic, which initiated much of the ensuing debate.

Sheehan, David. *The Children's Puzzle: A Study of Services to Children in Massachusetts.* Boston: University of Massachusetts Institute for Governmental Services, 1977.

Commissioned by the Massachusetts House Committee on Ways and Means, this report recommends that responsibility for the state's day care programs be transferred to the public schools.

Steiner, Gilbert Y. *The Children's Cause.* Washington, D.C.: The Brookings Institution, 1976.

Incisive and often caustic analysis of the "child development movement" during the late 1960s and early 1970s, which links the prospects of any national child care program to unemployment of teachers and to the efforts of the AFT on their behalf.

Steinfels, Margaret O'Brien. *Who's Minding the Children: The History and Politics of Day Care in America.* New York: Simon and Schuster, 1973.

Especially good history of the 19th century antecedents of current programs, along with thoughtful analysis of future issues for the development of any national child care policy, including the "public school question."

Sugarman, Jule M.; Martin, Edwin; and Taylor, Ted. "Who Will Deliver Education to Preschool Children?" In *One Child Indivisible,* edited by J. D. Andrews. Washington, D.C.: NAEYC, 1975.

Transcript of symposium at the 1974 NAEYC conference. Martin argues for presumed public school prime sponsorship; Sugarman and Taylor argue against it.

U.S. Congress, Senate Subcommittee on Children and Youth, Senate Subcommittee on Employment, Poverty, and Migratory Labor. House Subcommittee on Select Education. *Joint Hearings on the Child and Family Services Act, 1975,* 94th Congress, 1st session, March-July, 1975, 9 parts.

A key sourcebook for arguments in the debate about public school involvement in day care. Includes the testimony of most national organizations and individuals who joined the issue, such as Albert Shanker, Marian Wright Edelman, the National Black Child Development Institute, and AFSCME, as well as background papers on day care delivery, such as Hunsinger's and Kessler's "Child Care Policy: Maximizing Family Choice," originally prepared as a staff working paper for the Carnegie Council on Children.

IX.

Alphabet Soup: A Guide to Acronyms

Following is a decoding of acronyms which appear frequently in the text.

ACYF: Administration for Children, Youth, and Families. The new name for what used to be the Office of Child Development (OCD), the agency within the Department of Health, Education, and Welfare with responsibility for Head Start and for various aspects of federal day care programs.

AFDC: Aid to Families with Dependent Children. The major component of what is commonly referred to as "welfare," which provides income subsidy for the protection and care of young children.

AFL-CIO: American Federation of Labor—Congress of Industrial Organizations.

AFSCME: American Federation of State, County, and Municipal Employees. This large and influential union represents workers at all levels of government and advocates prime sponsorship by state and local units of government, not by the public schools.

AFT: American Federation of Teachers. In 1974, under the leadership of its President, Albert Shanker, this powerful teachers' union initiated the push for presumed public school prime sponsorship of any day care program to be developed under national legislation.

AISD: Austin Independent School District. Receives funds from the Texas Education Authority (TEA) for the Education for Parenthood Program, the day care component of which it administers jointly with Child, Inc., a private nonprofit child care provider in Austin.

ARC: Appalachian Regional Commission. Federal agency established during the mid-1960s to provide funds for a variety of community development programs in the "Appalachian Region," which runs as far north as New York State. Child development programs in the northwestern parts of South Carolina, profiled in this report, have been eligible for ARC funding.

CDA: Child Development Associate Consortium. Private nonprofit corporation composed of national associations all of which have a direct interest in the field of early childhood education and child development. Receives funding from ACYF to assess the competence of child care personnel and to grant credentials to those persons assessed as competent.

DCCDCA: Day Care and Child Development Council of America, Inc. This national membership organization, which provides technical assistance to a variety of day care programs and which is a major source for publications about day care, strongly opposes public school presumed prime sponsorship.

DHR: Department of Human Resources. The name in Georgia for what in some other states is referred to as the state department of social services or the welfare department.

DSS: Department of Social Services. Sometimes called the Welfare Department of the Department of Human Resources.

EEA: Emergency Employment Act. Federal legislation in 1971 which allowed states to hire the unemployed for a variety of public service programs. South Carolina Governor West allocated a portion of his state's money for the employment of child care workers.

FIDCR: Federal Interagency Day Care Requirements. Stipulates programmatic standards, such as staff/child ratio, which day care programs must meet in order to receive federal funds.

4C's: Community Coordinated Child Care.

G.E.D.: General Equivalency Diploma. Certificate indicating completion of education equivalent to graduation from high school. Often the G.E.D. is earned in adult education or external degree programs.

GMDCA: Greater Minneapolis Day Care Association. One of the many state and local day care associations throughout the country that have taken a strong stand against presumed public school prime sponsorship.

NABCD: National Association for Black Child Development. Dedicated specifically to the rights, care, and education of black children, this professional membership organization has taken a strong position against presumed public school prime sponsorship.

NACDE: National Association for Child Development in Education. This Washington-based lobby for the country's private for-profit preschool and day care programs opposes public school involvement.

NBCDI: National Black Child Development Institute. This Washington-based nonprofit membership organization, which plays an advocacy role on behalf of black children and their families and works to improve child development and child welfare programs, opposes presumed public school prime sponsorship.

NAEYC: National Association for the Education of Young Children. The largest professional membership organization concerned with the care and education of young children. Since 1974, every NAEYC annual conference has included debates, discussions, or symposiums on the "public school question."

NEA: National Education Association. Though not officially a union, NEA has the largest membership of any "teacher organization." Since NEA President James Harris testified in favor of public school presumed prime sponsorship in 1975, NEA has been relatively quiet about day care.

NFIE: National Foundation for the Improvement of Education. In 1977, this research arm of the NEA prepared a thorough review of data and issues, "Child Warfare or Early Childhood Education?" which also outlines the steps NEA would have to take to develop a "pro-active" rather than a "reactive" position regarding any significant public school role in early education. This inhouse document is still being considered by the NEA executive committee.

SSI: Supplemental Security Income.

TEA: Texas Education Authority. The state education agency in Texas which awarded a pilot grant to the Austin Independent School District for implementation of the Education for Parenthood project.

Title IV-A: This provision of the 1967 amendments to the Social Security Act of 1935 provided the major source of public funding for day care from 1967 to 1975. Designed to encourage state departments of welfare to develop day care services for children who met federal eligibility requirements, it offered a 3:1 match of federal to state dollars. Although Title IV-A funding was originally open-ended, in 1972 the Congress placed a $2.5 billion limit on annual funding of social services, with allocation of funds among the states on a population basis. The social services part of Title IV-A was superseded in late 1975 by Title XX.

Title XX: A block-grant program for social services which replaced the social services section of Title IV-A; the $2.5 billion limit remains, though eligibility requirements were changed and greater flexibility was given to the states to develop state social services plans. Title XX is now the major source of public funds for day care.

UAW: United Auto Workers. Opposes presumed prime sponsorship by the public schools.

ABOUT THE AUTHOR

James A. Levine, Research Associate at the Wellesley College Center for Research on Women, is a consultant on child care and social policy for the Ford Foundation and many other organizations. He has taught "Child Development and Social Policy" at Wellesley, and is on the summer faculty of the Wheelock College Advanced Seminars in Day Care Management. Before joining Wellesley, Mr. Levine was Executive Director of Great Brook Valley Comprehensive Child Care Services, Inc., in Worcester, Massachusetts, and served as a staff member at the Foundation for Child Development and the Bank Street College of Education's Day Care Consultation Service, both in New York City. Articles by Mr. Levine have appeared in *Psychology Today, Day Care and Early Education, Young Children, Working Woman,* and other magazines; his book about men and childrearing—*Who Will Raise the Children? New Options for Fathers (and Mothers)* [Bantam paperback]—won the 1976 Family Life Book Award of the Child Study Association of America. Mr. Levine lives with his wife and two children in Wellesley, Massachusetts, where he is president of the board of the Wellesley Community Children's Center.